MAN
With a
VAN

My Story

Drew
PRITCHARD

EBURY
PRESS

1

Ebury Press, an imprint of Ebury Publishing
20 Vauxhall Bridge Road
London SW1V 2SA

Ebury Press is part of the Penguin Random House group of companies
whose addresses can be found at global.penguinrandomhouse.com

Penguin
Random House
UK

First published by Ebury Press in 2021
This paperback edition published in 2022

www.penguin.co.uk

A CIP catalogue record for this book is available from the British Library

ISBN 9781529106749

Printed and bound in Great Britain by Clays Ltd, Elcograf S.p.A.

The authorised representative in the EEA is Penguin Random House
Ireland, Morrison Chambers, 32 Nassau Street, Dublin DO2 YH68

Penguin Random House is committed to a sustainable future
for our business, our readers and our planet. This book is
made from Forest Stewardship Council® certified paper.

This book is dedicated to my Grandmother, Winifred 'Nin' Alice Roberts, my mother Joan, Tom, Charlotte and Grace

And to all the teachers who said I'd amount to nothing …

CONTENTS

INTRODUCTION

About a year ago I was asked to write a book about who I am and how I got into the world of antiques, about some of my more memorable experiences and about my TV shows. I've been doing *Salvage Hunters* on Quest for the last ten years, and it's complemented by another series that shows how we restore the items I buy, as well as a third show about classic cars. Initially I wasn't sure, but in the end my desire to share this incredible business with as many people as possible outweighed any personal reservations.

This a business like no other. No two days are the same; it's exciting, diverse and gives an insight into not just when or how items of great beauty or value were made, but the lives of the people who made them. It's about specific artistic movements that echo periods in history when art and design mirrored what was going on in the world of politics, fashion and culture. That's the fascination, what I call the 'soul' of the trade, and I hope I can pass on some of what I've learned and something of my passion.

That passion began when I was eight years old in my hometown of Glan Conwy in North Wales, and I'm almost 50 now, but nothing has changed. I feel exactly the same as I did when my eyes were first opened to the possibilities offered by old, discarded junk that nobody wanted. I refer to those items as 'decorative salvage' (a phrase I think I coined, though I can't say for certain), and I'm on a never-ending search for inventory. This is a business that requires a revolving door when it comes to stock, not just for my Conwy showroom, but for a website with a customer base that spans the globe. The items I find on TV are bought with my own money. Nothing is done for show and if the TV cameras weren't rolling there would be no difference in the way I deal with the vendor. I'm always on the lookout for innovative stock and much of what we sell goes abroad. If I took my foot off the throttle for just a few days things would quickly go pear-shaped; it's a constant challenge to find quality antiques but without them there's no turnover and no profit.

I never buy anything I wouldn't be happy to have in my house and often that's where a piece resides until somebody wants to buy it. All my furniture is for sale, whether it's in the shop or at home; just the other day I got back from a trip looking forward to an evening on the sofa with Netflix, only to find there was no sofa.

Hunting down decorative salvage is a way of life I revere, and I encourage as many of you to get involved as possible. Since we've been doing the TV series, I've come across more and more people dabbling in buying and selling, and that's why I agreed to do the show in the first place. As far as I'm concerned, the greater the interest the better the trade will be, and I'm forever bumping into people looking for advice. To me it's simple: *if you have the passion follow it*. Don't copy anyone else (least of all me); create your own idea of what you want to achieve and get on with it. Don't be afraid of the setbacks. I spoke to a couple at a fair the other day who were just starting out, and were worried that one week they'd sold stacks of stuff and the next absolutely nothing. Welcome to the antiques business. It takes years to learn and, as you'll see, you have to roll with the punches.

CHAPTER 1

HUMBLE BEGINNINGS

By the time 55 alloy storage bins had been loaded into the van we were completely knackered. We weren't finished yet, though; before we left the Bradford linen mill, we'd added a couple of massive wicker baskets and an industrial trolley. We were satisfied; it had been a really good call (which is how the antiques trade refers to it when we're asked to show up and look at potential inventory) in one of those places you rarely see. There aren't many linen mills left but this one was thriving with over half a million metres of fabric sold every year, and I'd picked up some quality industrial furniture.

Back in the van I checked my phone, while T pulled out alongside a lorry that was hazing us with spray that might as well have come from a hosepipe. My long-term sidekick, I've known T since I was a boy in North Wales and he's an integral part of the TV show. It had been pissing with rain all week but that was nothing new. After so many years on the road we were used to torrential downpours and the motorway flooding.

'It's been a decent day, T,' I said.

'Van's full.' He was concentrating on the traffic. 'You'll make money on those bins, and I really like that trolley.'

It had been the best call we'd had in weeks and I was encouraged about another factory visit tomorrow. There wasn't much to do by way of restoration on the stuff we'd bought, just a bit of a clean-up really.

An hour later we left the motorway and found the hotel in Higher Bartle, near Preston. A beautiful old place and a far cry from my first few years on the road when a night away meant the back of the van and a burger from a kiosk in the lay-by. I checked in, dumped my bags and took a long, hot shower. After that I went down to have dinner with the rest of the crew. Tomorrow was Dan's last shoot as director on the show; he was still producing. The sound man Simon Jolly has been with me from the very first day of shooting, and for a long time it's been Sean or Steve wielding the camera.

After grabbing a pint, I sat down to update the website, already thinking about tomorrow. That's the buzz, the excitement, the sense of anticipation I have before we arrive at any call. It's the same today as it has been for as long as I can remember, an obsession that's shaped my entire life and something I love with a passion.

All this was on my mind because I had this book to write and didn't know where to begin. It was something I discussed with T when he came in from a precarious walk along the road with no pavement and no street lights. He's a year older than me; we're about the same build and cut from the same North Wales granite.

'We might need another van for tomorrow,' he stated. 'If so, I can sort it. So, tell me about this book then.'

I looked at him over my glasses. 'There's not much to tell yet. I really don't know how to get started.'

'Easy. Piccadilly Woods.'

'What?'

'Those old cars hanging in trees, remember? It must be forty years since we've been there.'

I remember how quiet the world was when T and I used to play football on the A470. Growing up in North Wales in the 1970s and 80s, there were no mobile phones or social media, and home computers were in their infancy. We made our own fun and, for me, that meant turning up what I thought were rusty treasures. From the age of eight, back in 1978, I was obsessed and had a way of finding beauty in things that others saw as worthless junk only fit for the skip. I was always turning up with old bits and pieces of bicycle or some piece of rusting military hardware. It started when we moved from Llandudno Junction to Glan Conwy and I had so much junk piling up my grandmother, 'Nin', referred to me as a 'shite-hawk'. A magnet for crap, I rarely came home without something someone else had thrown away.

We started scouring the local tip to see what kind of stuff we could salvage. You don't see those tips any more, but back in the 1970s most towns and villages had a local dump where people would toss their old washing machines, bikes or whatever. There were a few of us lads who used to hang out, mostly it was me and T, Daz-Babs, a big lad who acted tough but was actually a bit of a baby, and another lad called Tyd. We roamed Glan Conwy like a pack of wolves, hunting junk all hours of the day. Daz-Babs and I were obsessed, and much of what we recovered came from the Second World War. North Wales is a military area, with RAF Valley on Anglesey and MOD buildings dotted all over. Most had become a dumping ground and we came up with all kinds of stuff: gas masks, ammunition cases, knives and bayonets. Daz-Babs amassed a huge collection of old bayonets and a lot of the older lads had guns from the period they would use to shoot ducks on the river. Glan Conwy is on an estuary and another source of junk was the sea. With constant tides there was always a good deal of debris washing up – oars, old water skis, bits of boat – and we'd comb the beach for anything interesting we could recover.

Going to the woods, though, that had been a dare not a salvage hunt. They were scary and particularly to an eight-year-old boy like me. It was already getting dark and we were supposed to be going home, but one of the lads suggested we check them out so off we went, Daz-Babs, Tyd, T and me. A developer had been building a new housing estate that wasn't finished yet, and we picked our way between piles of bricks and scaffolding. Beyond it the woodland was really thick and we had to forge a path until we came to a point where the hills grew up on either side of this massive V-shaped valley. Both sides were covered in trees that were so dense I could barely see. As I stared into the gloom, however, I began to make out something my eight-year-old brain could not get to grips with. Cars, loads of them, ancient rusty relics, seemed to be hanging in midair like ghosts of what they'd been.

It was the most amazing sight I'd ever seen. I didn't understand it at first but, as we got closer, I was able to figure it out. The cars weren't ghosts and they weren't hanging in the air, they were jammed between the edge of the V-shaped ravine and the trees. I got it: people had pushed their unwanted cars to the edge of the hill above and let them roll down into the V. Many had smashed into the trunks of trees and, as the years went by and the trees grew taller, so the cars grew with them until they were hoisted into the air. I was amazed. This was magical. There were cars from the 1930s and 40s, some going back as far as the Model T. A graveyard for old vehicles, they rested as if on burial scaffolds, smothered by the leaves of trees. What I saw wasn't a bunch of knackered old wrecks, though, it was beauty, history, money; as well as a sense of time and place that I'd never otherwise have seen.

It was exciting, exhilarating, the most incredible experience of my life so far. Not only that, I think that deep down I knew there was money to be made from the bits and pieces we might find there. We started rummaging around, but it was spooky, pretty dark and hard to see. The next day we were back, climbing into the trees to see what we could salvage. Most of the cars had been there for decades and were rusted to hell. It was lethal so we really had to take care (but didn't) and I set about prising badges from bonnets, ripping off old hub caps, gear knobs, anything I thought deserved to be saved and things I might be able to get a couple of quid for.

From then on, the passion really took hold. I would spend every waking moment thinking about what kind of stuff might be out there and I also started to read. My dad was an artist, a sign-writer by trade, and both he and Mum had an interest in antiques. They had a few Lyle books on antiques dotted around the house so I picked them up and began to read. Armed with a little bit of knowledge, I started finding old tins and boxes and they weren't just beautiful, they were useful. I could keep things in boxes but they had to be ones that really caught my eye. There was a scrapyard in Llandudno Junction that I used to hang around outside. As soon as it closed and everyone had gone, I'd jump over the fence and get lost in a wonderful world of my own. I wasn't there to nick anything, just to have a really good look around.

I have no idea why I became so obsessed, but I'm no different today. Doing what I do, travelling around the world locating things that otherwise might never be recovered, allows me a glimpse into the lives of the people that made them. The past comes to life in both time and place, and I get a sense of why someone decided to make something, paint something, build something that would outlive not only them, but me.

I was inspired by things that people just didn't appear to see. It was the same with the other lads. If one of us got word of an old bike in some shed in the middle of nowhere, or some derelict car somewhere, we would cycle for miles just to go and take a look at it. It was the only thing that interested me, aged stuff, things that had been made long ago. I always used to think about who had made them and why. I was fascinated by the history, the stories behind the stuff itself. It occupied my mind from the moment I woke to the moment I went to sleep. Nothing else seemed to matter. Certainly not school. I only studied if I was interested in the subject and that didn't include many of my lessons. I was there in body (most of the time) but never in spirit. I was learning nothing at all.

School did have its advantages though; from the age of ten or eleven, I started dealing in dinner tickets bought by our parents for 65p apiece. I'd buy them off other kids for 35p and sell them for 50p. Sometimes I'd swap them for cigarettes, which I'd sell on to buy air pistols and hunting knives, catapults, even pushbikes. Dr Marten boots were a favourite; pretty quickly I had quite the inventory and I realised I had a natural aptitude for buying and selling.

CHAPTER 1

By this time, I had a shed in the garden my dad said I could use to keep all the stuff I was collecting. As a child I didn't go without, but a lot of the time the stuff I got was reworked and second-hand; a bike, for example, would never be new, as my parents were far from rolling in money. There was never quite enough to spread to the luxuries and that hung over the household like a cloud. It bothered me. I didn't want to be like that. I wanted to have more than 'enough' money and was determined to find a way to achieve that. I didn't know it then, but it would turn out to be from finding old bits and pieces of what looked like junk, but to me was opportunity. From a really early age, I would hunt down old bits and pieces of bicycle, fix them up and sell them from the side of the road.

Back then Dad was working from the house, sign-writing a lot of vans, and some of those vans belonged to antique dealers. Whenever they showed up, I noticed it was in top-of-the-line Range Rovers or Mercedes. I was already into cars, and by the time I was 15 I had 13 motors I was breaking up for spares. They took up all the garden and most of the wood next door. Our house was on the A470 with a large sloping wood out the back that drifted down the hill towards the estuary. People started to complain and, finally, someone from the council came to the house.

'Mrs Pritchard,' they said, when Mum opened the door, 'your son's running a scrapyard from your garden and that's not allowed.'

'Don't be so stupid.' She was vehement. 'Of course he's not, he's only a child.' She sent him off with a flea in his ear and slammed the door.

A little later I came in from school and she collared me in the kitchen. 'Drew, you're running a scrapyard and the council have been round. You have to get rid of the cars.'

There was nothing to be done so I enlisted the help of my mates and we literally pushed 13 cars onto trailers or down to the local scrapyard. All save one, that was reserved for the council. They'd put an end to a lucrative business, so one night we pushed it all the way to their offices and left it outside the main door.

With this fledgling business totally screwed, I was really pissed off and became even more disruptive at school, Ysgol Dyffryn Conwy in Llanrwst, which was a few miles from where we lived in Glan Conwy. It was a co-ed where the pupils were streamed into sets T, S, M, F and K depending on ability and application. They were just letters with no real significance, but we named them Top, Second, Middle, Fick and Kretins. I was in F for Fick. I wasn't thick, I just didn't try. I completely understood what the teachers were telling me, but I knew I'd never use any of it so what was the point of learning about oxbow lakes or the life cycle of an amoeba? I was bored shitless and I made that known to anyone and everyone. In the end I was so bad, so disruptive to the other kids and teachers, one of them sat me down.

'Pritchard,' he said, 'you've got to listen to what I tell you. That's the point of a lesson, you know.'

I looked at him with a derisive eye. 'Why should I listen to you, sir? You've got a shit job. I know exactly what I'm going to do when I leave and it's got nothing to do with anything you can teach me.'

That was my attitude; I had no interest at all and during the five years I was there I think I did my homework once. Of course, that wasn't acceptable, but they couldn't give me detention because we lived ten miles away and detention meant missing the bus. They had to do something though; and in those days there was still the cane so I took that and carried on just as before. I had absolutely no interest in academia; school just got in the way of what I wanted to do, which was to get out on my own. By the time the council took those cars off me, I'd already left school (mentally at least), but they made me stay another year. I knew what I wanted to do, I wanted to be an antique dealer, but I had no clue how to go about it. Those guys that showed up at home in their posh Range Rovers were always really interesting people. Loads of laughter and jokes; they seemed to really enjoy what they were doing and that's where I wanted to be.

Those memories seemed to resonate again as T and I went to join the rest of the crew at the table Dan had reserved so we could watch the latest episode of the show on TV. It was a good show, well put together, and I was happy with it, though I hate to see myself on screen; it's something I only do once for each show, when the episode first airs, so I can be around to answer any questions that might come up on social media. Ours is an interactive process: we have 19 million viewers covering 32 countries around the world, so it's important I'm on hand to reply to any comments or questions.

I slept pretty well and the following morning T and I set out for the day's filming in Chorley, an old Lancashire mill town between Wigan, Blackburn and Preston. Back in the day it would have been tall, brick chimneys raking the skyline as far as the eye could see. For generations the local factory was the centre of the community, with terraces of houses built all around it. Most are long gone now, with only a few dotted around, and one was the Droyt Soap Company, the factory we were going to visit.

It was established in Minsk, Belarus, in 1893, so I was keen to learn how the factory came to be in Chorley. It's not just the buying and selling that fascinates me, though I love that, of course; there's nothing better than spotting an item, making an offer and selling it at a profit. That's what we do but it's not the whole story. More than the money it's the soul of an item that gets me. Recently, I bought a lady's rocking chair from the 1840s. Many of these were normal four-legged chairs that were later modified with rockers, but this had been made specifically. I paid a lot of money for it, but with a little restorative care I'll sell it for a lot more. But that wasn't my motivation when I first saw it. I wondered who had made it, who sat in it, how many times it had been bought and sold. I thought about all the stories that chair could tell if only it could talk; almost two hundred years of history, including two world wars that it seemed to have survived unscathed. That's the real excitement of this business, and there was always the chance I'd come across that kind of gem today.

It was a little tight manoeuvring the van through the narrow streets, but we found the factory surrounded by houses. A true product of the Industrial Revolution with grilles over the windows, ancient brickwork that was so black and weather-beaten it looked like the place had been empty for years. But it wasn't; it was a thriving business selling to major retailers in the UK as well as far-flung places like Japan. After parking the van in the yard out back, we went around to the front and knocked on the panel door. A couple of minutes later it was opened by a tall, slim man who'd arranged the call.

'Alistair?' I said.

He nodded.

'I'm Drew. This is T. Nice to meet you.'

'Nice to meet you too,' he said. 'I'm the sales director. Welcome to the Droyt Soap Company.'

He led us into a pretty spectacular room with flagstone floor and cast-iron columns holding up a pitched ceiling made from old timber that reminded me of my first warehouse in Builder Street, Llandudno, which I bought in about 2005. This was a remnant of days long past, part of that Industrial Age you no longer see. As he pointed out the features, Alistair explained that the building started life in Victorian times as a cotton yarn mill while Droyt was being founded in Minsk. Before the company moved to Chorley, the original factory was relocated to the banks of the Volga River in Saratov. After the Russian Revolution it moved again, this time to Berlin. It seemed that war and social unrest was a big part of their history because they switched to Chorley a couple of years before the outbreak of the Second World War.

This was the only factory left round here, but there had been another across the road. That firm manufactured plastic tape, and between the two was an old lodge with foundations so rotten the place perpetually filled up with water. It got so bad that, finally, something was done and a firm of experts was brought in to drain the water away before the lodge could be demolished. When it was gone, they discovered a colony of two thousand frogs that had to be taken to a nearby nature reserve. Thinking of all those frogs lurking in the darkness, I was keen to take a look at what might be hiding here. That would have to wait a moment, though, because the first thing that struck me wasn't the original flags or pillars, it was the sound of a machine: *Bang, Bang – Bang. Bang, Bang – Bang. Bang, Bang – Bang.*

It bounced off the walls like an echo, mimicking the beat of the Queen anthem 'We Will Rock You'. In a far corner, three women in blue overalls and white mesh caps were gathered at a stamping machine. They explained that the soap had been dried and, cut and now they were stamping it into moulds. *Bang, Bang – Bang.*

Everywhere I looked there was soap, massive blocks of it, orange, blue and green; they had to be a metre and a half in length and at least half a metre thick. Alistair pointed out where the old weaving shed had been when this was a cotton mill. He explained that, when the factory was adapted from yarn to soap, the vats were fired by an old coal boiler that had to be lit by a specialist every day. The coal explained why the bricks outside were so black; this place had been coughing out columns of smoke for decades. Looking up at the ancient timber rafters I was reminded again of my first warehouse in Llandudno. I wish I hadn't sold it, but it was the usual story of an offer you can't refuse.

The place smelled of soap (of course it did, what else would it smell of? It was a soap factory) but it wasn't overpowering and not unpleasant. Alistair explained that the smell is supposed to fade when you wash, because soap is designed to do no more than leave you clean so you can splash on some cologne.

'They are scented, of course,' he said. 'The blocks. The orange one is mandarin, the green lime and basil.'

One of the crew piped up: 'What scent would a Drew Pritchard soap be?'

'Curry powder,' T said. 'Or lager.'

'Expensive lager,' I corrected.

Something had caught my eye, the first thing I'd seen here that I thought I might be able to buy. Just beyond the massive blocks of soap was an industrial cutting table. About the size of a small dining table, it was seriously over-engineered with legs made from folded steel. The surface was zinc plate mounted on timber planks, well used and worn with a nicely aged patina. It wouldn't need much doing to it other than a proper clean. I checked the legs and the welding really was 'belt and braces'. Alistair told me the table had been made by some ex-employees, and that's always a nice back story. I can sell tables like that all day long; this was something I wanted to buy.

'It really is over-engineered,' I said. 'But I love the look. I love the zinc top.' I tried to lift it. 'How much does it weigh?'

'A hundred and twenty kilos.'

About what I expected given the heavy-steel construction. 'Is it something you'd sell?'

'Yes,' Alistair said. 'I think so.'

'What d'you want for it?' I took another look at the zinc, working my thumb over the greasy surface. 'What's a new one going to cost you?'

Alistair considered the table. 'I don't know,' he said. 'The last time we replaced one, it was a hundred and eighty pounds.'

The table had something going on and I was keen to have it. 'Alright,' I said. 'How much d'you want for it?' I was thinking about what I was prepared to pay and hoping we could come to an agreement. 'When I first started selling things like this thirty years ago, there was quite a lot of industrial stuff around but not so much now.' I stood back with a hand in my pocket. 'That makes a difference to the price. But I like it. What do you think?'

Alistair was quiet for a moment. 'All the others we have are stainless steel. This is zinc.'

'So, what're you telling me? If I buy it and start cleaning – it's going to bubble up?' We laughed, but it happens all the time. Alistair assured me it was cleaned every day with a special paraffin-based solution.

'I'll give you two-fifty,' I told him. 'Can't do any more. That's it.'

We shook on it. Deal done, the first of a few, I was hoping. A little back and forth on the price as usual, but I'd made him a decent offer and he took it. When I buy something, more often than not I'm taking a chance because I'm working off a gut feeling and not much more. Any research that might add value is done after. Even now, these deals are done on a handshake: old-school trust between two people who come to an amicable arrangement; even extremely large deals are done that way.

I wasn't sure there would be big-ticket stuff here, and so far I'd only bought one item and was keen to find some more. I had a vanload of largish items from Bradford, so when Alistair brought out some old brass soap stamps, I was delighted. What we call smalls – less-expensive items that are vital to the business, keep the cashflow going and don't take up a lot of room. These stamps weren't that old but they had something about them. The engineering in particular, the way the stamp slotted so perfectly into the mould, really got me.

'I'd love to buy some of these,' I said. 'I'd like to buy them all, in fact. Are any for sale?'

They were made of bronze, which in itself isn't that expensive, but the casting, the artwork, clearly was. There was one for 'Lagerfeld', another for 'Heal's' and 'Liberty'; there was even one for 'Burger King'. Great ornamental pieces, I knew they'd walk out the door.

'Are any for sale?' I repeated.

Alistair wasn't sure. The stamps were part of the history of his company and I liked the fact he felt that was important. There was as much of a story in some of the stuff in this factory as there was in the rocking chair I mentioned before.

'You can't flog these ones, can you?' I indicated those with the moulds that seemed to slot together so perfectly.

'No, I can't. They're an important part of the company.'

'What about the others?' I pointed to the individual stamps without moulds. 'Which of these can you let go?' I had a couple between my fingers now, holding them like knuckle dusters. 'Obviously, you don't have to, but I'd like to buy them if you want to.'

He was prepared to sell some of those and after a little deliberation we settled on three, so I asked Alistair what he wanted.

'I suppose it depends on what it would cost to have a new one made.' He pointed out the 'Lagerfeld'. 'That one would be at least two hundred pounds.'

I shook my head. 'That's not going to happen; I can't give you two hundred pounds for all three. Best I can do is a hundred.'

'For all three?'

I nodded.

Alistair thought about that. 'Alright,' he said, and we shook on it.

This was good – a table and some smalls, and I hadn't paid too much. This kind of stuff is easy to sell and there was room for a decent profit. Alistair was needed by one of his staff, so I took the opportunity to check back with the showroom in Conwy, where someone was making an offer on a piece on the website I'd priced at just under £4,000. I had to look twice as the offer was so far off, I thought they must've typed in the wrong number. I asked one of the girls back in Conwy to check on that and make sure I got back to it later.

Having dealt with the request from his staff, Alistair took us up a very steep flight of stairs to another large production room, then into what he described as 'The Lab', a section full of chemicals and bottles of soap solution beyond a partition made from hand-made wooden boxes. A line about six metres long by two high, they had been nailed together like pigeon holes. The boxes originated in Argentina, where they had been lined with greaseproof paper and filled with liquid beef tallow which would cool and set before the lid was nailed on. Beef tallow had been an integral part of the soap-making process before BSE – mad cow disease – hit in the 1980s. In those days the three main components were the tallow, castor oil and coconut oil. Post-BSE, the beef tallow has been replaced with palm oil.

'Are they for sale?' I asked him. 'The boxes? I'd like to buy the lot.'

'No, they're part of the business, not to mention the wall.'

I hadn't been very hopeful, and shipping them without taking the boxes apart would have posed a few problems, but that was nothing we couldn't get over. No matter, already I'd spotted a couple of wooden boards with cast-iron hasps on the underside that had been used to stack blocks of soap. They would be great for someone's kitchen, food preparation or display. Alistair said he'd take 50 quid for the pair.

'No, that's undervaluing them,' I told him. 'I'll give you sixty.'

He seemed pleased with that and I took another look at the boxes. Ox-blood in colour, they would've made a great display somewhere and I knew there would be a market for them. But I had to be content with the soap stands and another bronze. From a metal cupboard Alistair brought out a whole stack of individual crafted moulds of various shapes and sizes. There were ducks, birds, cartoon characters – I'd have snapped them all up. That wasn't going to happen, though; these were pretty old, some dating back to the 1920s in Berlin and others that had been made when the factory moved to Chorley. I asked if they would let any go and Alistair offered me one mould of a sailor. His name was Jack and I could sell stuff like this easily enough, but I knew the retail price was only a couple of hundred quid. This was another bespoke piece and to replace it with something else that was hand-crafted would cost a couple of thousand. The only reason Alistair was prepared to sell at all was because the mould bore the 'Droyt' name and that was good marketing. I wanted it, but unless I spent money on the way it was displayed, I knew I couldn't get more than 200 quid. I had to think. I couldn't make him a ridiculous offer, but I had to take a chance. 'What about a hundred and forty?'

He was happy to take that, so Jack the Sailor was added to the inventory.

There were only a few items and we managed to squeeze them into the van, which saved the cost and bother of bringing down another. Job done we set off for Conwy in the driving rain. Today was Thursday, I'd been on the road all week, tomorrow I'd be in the shop then it was off again on Saturday.

'Remind me where we're going next week,' I said before we pulled out of the narrow gates.

T stopped the van and checked the call sheet before we continued. 'Sunday it's the flea market at Shepton Mallet. Then Dorset and Wiltshire.' We set off and he glanced across the cab as we came to the junction. 'On Saturday you said you were going to Bath, so I'll have to meet you after.'

The call to Bath Dec Fair wasn't for the TV show, it was purely business. There were dealers I needed to see. Right now, though, I'd have a breather, so I let T find our way back to the motorway. Before long, we were on the M6, with rain lashing the windscreen. 'Another pretty good day,' I said. 'I'm happy, T: we bought some good stuff today.'

'What're you going to do with the mould?'

'Jack the Sailor? Mount him, of course, what else would I do?'

Back home Gavin, my full-time restorer who's been with me for years, unloaded the van, and then I went to take Enzo for a walk. My beloved Jack Russell, he was getting pretty long in the tooth, but there's no better way of dusting off the cobwebs than taking your dog along the beach, regardless of the pouring rain. Unfortunately, he's gone now, having passed away while I was working on this book, and I miss him terribly. While he was sniffing around checking his wee-mails, I was thinking about tomorrow and Bath. I'd go by myself, take the 'posh van' (Range Rover) because that was big enough to load some stuff in the back, then I'd meet up with the TV crew in time for the shoot on Sunday. It struck me then that, despite all the setbacks, I'd achieved what I set out to do. The posh van was what the dealers who showed up at our house turned up in when I was a boy and now I had one as well.

It's things like that, and the other cars I've owned, that remind me how far I've come since that moment with the lads in Piccadilly Woods. It's not just the money, though, it's the business I'd set my heart on being a part of.

Only just done with school, I was a long way from being any kind of dealer and just as far from driving a Range Rover. I had the grand total of 12p in my pocket and no idea what I was going to do. I had a little bit of knowledge from reading catalogues and books, but the reality was the antiques business was like the Mafia. There was just no way in for a lad from Glan Conwy like me. Those guys didn't want anyone around with even half a brain cell; they wanted lads who could hump stuff, load it onto vans. There was no way I could get a job in the antiques trade and I was a bit scared to even ask. I had to do something, though, so, for some reason I'll never be able to explain, I decided to join the RAF. Luckily, I didn't get in. Given my record of attendance at school, it surprised no one (least of all me) when I missed an interview and that was the end of it, thank God.

Things changed when Dad finished a sign-writing job for Gordon Stewart, a local stained-glass restorer who operated out of an old farm above Abergele with another guy called Joe Sturges. By then my dad and I were no longer getting on, and our relationship was only going to get worse. For reasons I don't think I'll ever understand, things were pretty strained, and he didn't think I'd ever amount to anything. He wasn't going to let me sit around, though – not that I would – and when Gordon turned up at the house to pick up his van, they got talking about his business.

'You haven't got a job for my son, have you?' Dad said. 'He's fucking useless, doing nothing right now.'

'I might.' Gordon looked me up and down like I was some bull at a farm auction. Back then I was quite muscly. I used to play a lot of rugby, and rode a BMX bike everywhere. I was fit and strong.

'You look like you can lift a box of lead. Can you?'

'Yeah,' I said. 'Of course.'

'Alright, then. Monday morning.'

I was up for it, a job in the stained-glass window restoring business, it might just be a way into a world I never thought I'd have a chance to crack. I arrived early courtesy of a lift from Mum as I was only 16 and not yet driving. Gordon put me to work in what was called the 'Cementing Shed': a filthy little room, he pointed out a leaded window, the lead light cement etc., then told me to get the brush and use it to put the cement into the gap. When it was dry, I was to rub the top layer off so just the lead was left. It didn't seem too hard so I set about it and I was meticulous. I wasn't unhappy. I wasn't in school. I was on the YTS (Youth Training Scheme) getting £17.40 a week, which was a fortune to me, so I got stuck in.

A couple of days later a van showed up in the yard that had been sign-written 'Michael Maine Architectural Antiques' by my dad. This miserable-looking guy got out and called to me across the yard.

'Oi, boy! Come here and give us a hand.' He indicated the back doors.

I went to help unload and, when the doors were opened, I found myself staring at a load of different items that really caught my eye. I saw a wooden front door with butterflies painted into the stained glass. I saw old fireplaces, picture frames, bits of stone sill. Like someone had snapped their fingers or a light going on in my head, it was a Eureka moment, the first of a few I would have in my life. That's it, I thought. This is exactly where I want to be. I remember walking back into the cementing shed and closing the door. I remember looking at the piece I was working on, aware of all the knowledge I'd already amassed and thinking, Right, let's have this. This is what I'm going to do.

The very next day Gordon took me to a church that was being knocked down in Holyhead on Anglesey. The demolition contractor wanted all the stained-glass windows taken out as he planned to keep them. I learned how to take those windows out on the job, which was another great thing to do. When we were finished, we piled them into the guy's van and I thought no more about it as we drove back to Abergele.

CHAPTER 2

VOYAGE TO VINLAND

The day after I got home from Chorley, I was off early for the stop in Bath on my way to the flea market at Shepton Mallet. It was quite nice to be driving myself. I don't get to do it often, for years it's been me and T. The car is something of an office, though, and as I drove south, I had the phone plugged in, making call after call to keep the business rolling. When I got to the Bath Decorative Antiques Fair, I hooked up with the dealers I wanted to see and filled up the car with stock. After that it was a short hop to the Premier Inn at Frome where I met T and the rest of the TV crew.

By Sunday morning the rain that had plagued us all last week had finally packed in. It had been replaced by single-figure temperatures and a freezing wind that was buffeting across the country. The crew went ahead while T and I checked the van. When we were ready it was 12 miles through twisting country roads to the flea market at the Royal Bath Showground just outside Shepton Mallet. Even though it was bloody freezing, I was looking forward to the day. Flea markets can be hit and miss but this was usually a good one. For the last 20 years it's been run by Kate Ede, who was also behind the Decorative Fair in Bath where I'd been yesterday. Most of the stands are set up inside this massive, modern arena, something like 240 of them with another 200 outside. I make a point of visiting them all so we were going to be here all day.

No messing around, I walked the stalls with T, starting inside the arena and moving swiftly, the film crew following behind us. After so many years in the business my senses are pretty well tuned and I only stop if something really grabs my attention. It wasn't long before I spotted a hint of brass that appealed to me straightaway. A dealer from Odiham in Hampshire had a pair of three-tier Italian etageres, free-standing shelves for displaying books or ornaments; these two looked to be from the late 1950s. Made of brass, the shelves themselves were what T and I decided to term 'Lino-flux'. They had a linoleum feel to them, but despite that I knew I could make good money. The dealer wanted £700 for the pair. I checked them over, no work to be done, the kind of thing I'd get a grand for, maybe 1,100.

'I'll give you six for the two.'

It was a good start, the first purchase of the day, I always like to get that out of the way. Outside we were in a biting wind that was so fierce half the items on the stalls seemed to be blowing away. I had to duck to avoid an old watering can that went flying as a gust sent it clattering across our path. We moved from stall to stall, though I stopped to speak to people on the way. Many of the people who attend these fairs also watch the show. It's funny, I was never someone who wanted to be recognised (and still don't). It can go either way. Sometimes I walk into a room somewhere and every person knows who I am. At the same time, I can buy a cup of coffee in a crowded petrol station and nobody has a clue.

That stretch of stalls outside the main warehouse was heaving. There was some pretty good stuff around, some of it from dealers I knew. After stopping to chat to a few people who wanted selfies, I prised myself loose from one woman who left a big smacker on my cheek. T had spotted an articulated industrial lamp sitting on top of an ancient bar-football table, so I went over to take a look. I buy a lot of these lamps, they always sell well, but this wasn't in the best of condition and the price was more than I wanted to pay.

Switching from stall to stall, we paused at one where the dealer was selling everything from riding boots on shoe trees to ancient dustbins and books. Nothing there really caught my eye so we carried on. Up ahead I could see some metal chairs that looked interesting. They were being sold by a young guy from the back of a van but the wind was blowing so hard the path between the stalls was a maelstrom of flying bits and pieces. I liked the look of those chairs, though, so I took a closer look and asked the guy where he was from.

'Frome,' he said. 'Just up the road. My name's Chris.'

'I'm Drew,' I said. 'This is T. Are you a dealer?'

'No, I'm not a dealer. I sell coffee for a living. The chairs are from my shop.'

They were Tolix, designed by Xavier Pauchard, from Saint Leger in France, who died in 1948. Brand new these were 250 apiece and Chris wanted 120 for the pair.

'I'll take them,' I said.

Another quick and easy buy. No point messing around, I could double my money with nothing needed but a rudimentary clean.

This was going better than I'd thought. There was some nice stuff here; I picked up a confit pot for 15 quid and an old educational canvas poster for 60.

'Not a bad day so far,' T said as we headed for a dealer with a large steel potting table as well as a garden bench.

'Yeah, we've got some nice pieces, particularly those etageres.' I considered the potting table but there was a tag of 800 quid on it and the dealer was Elizabeth Lee. I knew she'd want that all day long and it was too rich for me.

'The bench, T: what do you think?'

'Nicely weathered,' he said.

'It's a Lutyens. He was an architect, but he designed a specific bench for a garden somewhere and this is a copy.'

'She's asking two-fifty,' T said.

I nodded. 'I've bought off her before and she's bought off me. No point pissing about, I can get four-fifty at least.' I took another good look at the bench. 'Ironic I should find this now. A year ago, Diane Keaton asked me for two Lutyens but I couldn't find one anywhere.'

'Diane Keaton the actress?'

'Yeah, she bought a lamp off me for her kitchen years ago. Now there's a woman with taste. You should see her houses; she's got the kind of eye most dealers would kill for.'

I shook hands on the deal with Elizabeth and told her we'd be back for the Lutyens later. As I said before, a handshake is the way this business is done and that was for 250 quid, but the antiques trade knows no boundaries and you can shake on tens of thousands.

An early experience of that was at my very first Newark Antiques Fair in 1993, which was mammoth compared to Shepton Mallet. By then I'd lost my job with Gordon Stewart, having spent seven years learning the restoration business. It was Christmas Eve in 1993 when he showed up unannounced at our house. I remember seeing him pull up outside and rubbing my hands, thinking, Christmas bonus, lovely. But that's not why he was there. He sat down looking drawn and pale, then told me that Michael Maine, his biggest customer, had gone bust on him and the knock-on effect meant Gordon had lost his house. He had lost everything, in fact. He couldn't pay me. I was 23 years old and no longer had a job.

After he'd gone, I remember sitting there wondering what I was going to do. All I had was 200 quid and an old VW Beetle with a roof rack. It was a bit of a shock. I didn't blame Gordon, I owe him a lot; under his tutelage I'd gone from the cement shed to being a highly skilled restorer, involved in major projects and design within the company. But, perhaps just as importantly, I'd encouraged him to start selling bits of stained glass, which he really couldn't be arsed to do. Now that came into play. Before he left, Gordon told me he couldn't pay me what was owed, but there was one last thing he could do. Back at the farm there was an old bull-pit where we used to store all the crap. Old doors, window frames, etc. that we'd dump after we'd salvaged the glass. Gordon said I could have whatever I wanted. It wasn't very inspiring. I knew what was there, a knackered old cupboard door with little art-nouveau windows, some door handles, bits of fireplaces, panelling; a whole load of shit, but it was my only option and I was sure there was something I could do with it.

Long ago I'd learned that what's shit to someone else is a thing of beauty to me, and I knew exactly what I was going to do. The very next day I set up 'Classical Glass', which was a rubbish name, but all I could think of at the time. My first proper business venture: seven years after unloading Michael Maine's van I had absolutely no clue how to do anything, but I'd have a go. What I did have was some knowledge and experience of antique dealers, having been working with them for the last few years. I suppose I was 'in the mix'. I knew one lad in particular from Manchester called Carl for whom I'd been doing a bit of restoration work. He had a door-stripping business and a barn where he sold stuff, which seemed like a really big deal to me. He was my first port of call, a phone call on a land line (no mobiles in those days), asking if he wanted any old stained glass. He said he'd take a look, so I piled all I could salvage from the bull-pit into my Beetle and drove to Manchester. And 450 quid later, I left his place with an empty Beetle, thinking, That's it, I'm off. I'm in.

Over a brew we'd had a long chat and Carl told me he was looking for 'top-light' windows, as many as I could find, and he'd give me a fiver apiece. They had just put the A55 road through North Wales, linking Colwyn Bay, Rhyl and Abergele, so I had a corridor to play with. A few days later I put a small advert in the *North Wales Weekly News*:

Wanted — Stained Glass & Architectural Antiques. Cash Paid. Any Amount. Anywhere

I gave my parents' home number as the contact and the phone just rang off the hook. Back then, I was the only guy in North Wales buying glass and various other bits of salvage so every time a demolition came up the contractor would be on the phone. I had the whole of Anglesey and the Conwy Valley. Most of my mates from school were either builders or plumbers, and every Friday we'd meet up for a pint. Invariably, they'd tell me about a marble bath or sink they were stripping out of some old property somewhere.

Pretty quickly I found myself looking at a massive hoard of windows that had come off another old church. I had to buy this stuff and pay cash. The problem was, I'd bought a crappy Astra van and all I had to my name now was 300 quid. Somehow, I had to persuade these people to give me all that glass. Fortunately, I had some negotiation skills from my days bartering for dinner tickets and knocking on doors for old cars when I was a kid. That experience would come in handy now. I bought the broken pieces of glass for a pound each and the good ones for three quid.

For 18 months I worked with Carl, supplying not just the glass but old fireplaces and other bits and pieces I came across. I had a small restoration business. I was selling to other people here and there and all of it in cash. One day after I'd dropped off a load of top-lights, Carl asked if I knew about the Newark Antiques Fair.

'Sure,' I said. 'I've heard of it, but I've never been.'

'Go,' he said. 'Take everything you've got and charge triple what you charge me.'

He didn't need to tell me that. He just reiterated what I already knew, but in articulating it like that he did me a massive favour and I'll always thank him for that.

The fact was I had a lot of stuff; it was everywhere. I was renting garages, I had junk with friends all over the place. I'd moved out of my parents' house into a two-up, two-down in the middle of Conwy, and it was like a mini-warehouse. I had stuff in every room. I still had loads at my parents' place as well as my grandmother's and some of it was pretty good. There was some really nice eighteenth-century oak panelling I'd found on a farm above Abergele. I had a stack of arched church windows, tons of lead lights; far too much for the Astra, so I hired a 7.5 tonne truck.

Loaded to the gunwales, I drove across country to Newark, having never handled that kind of vehicle before. The fair was an eye-opener, amazing, with over five thousand stalls. It lasted three days and I couldn't afford anywhere to stay so I made some room in the back of the van, unrolled a sleeping bag and ate baked beans out of the can. I spent the night back there and by dawn I was raring to go. This was exciting, the anticipation incredible. I had no idea what to expect but I knew what I was going to do. Triple the prices, Carl had said, but there seemed to be so much money around I thought I could do better than that. Dragging all the stuff out of the van, I got set up and, by the 5:30am start, I was ready to go.

It was brutal, full-on; back then the antiques trade was still making massive money. That first morning it was trade only, and within a few minutes of my laying everything out an American dealer stopped and pointed to a window.

'How much?'

I looked it over, thinking I'd normally get 100 quid.

'Fifteen hundred,' I said.

'I'll take it. Have you got any more?'

'Four.'

'OK, I'll take them all.'

A little while later, Bob Mills (who used to run Robert Mills Antiques) rolled up and offered me eight grand for a bunch of other windows. He wrote a cheque, which I didn't want to take, having never had one before. But I spoke to another dealer and he told me a cheque from Bob was OK.

It just went on from there. In less than an hour I made more money than I'd earned in my entire life. A German guy came by and offered me £1,200 for the oak panelling, which I accepted. I had a pair of massive stained-glass windows that had come from a chapel that was demolished in Bangor, and they went as well.

That first day at Newark I started running out of stock and there were still two more days to go. So off I went to get some more with my pockets so full of cash I waddled from stall to stall. I started buying all sorts of stuff, working on the instinct I'd been developing every day since I was a kid, and it stood me in good stead when it came to trusting my eye. It really was the beginning of something, my first trade-fair experience, and I came away not just happy, but eager and hungry for more.

Things moved on, and a year or so after that first pitch at Newark I was working from an inspection pit under my dad's garage at the house where I grew up in Glan Conwy. It was a tiny little space we'd partitioned with a single, head-height window. By then I'd employed a lad called Darren who I was teaching to restore in the same way Gordon Stewart and Joe Sturges had taught me back when I was doing my apprenticeship. I'd spent seven years learning the stained-glass business and I'd kept up on the reading: books, magazines, catalogues from bygone auctions. They're stacked floor to ceiling at home. Even now the last thing I do at night before I go to sleep is read about antiques. The first thing I do when I wake up in the morning is read about antiques. Back then I'd done a lot of research into William Morris. He and Edward Burne-Jones were artists and designers heavily involved in re-energising the British stained-glass tradition back in the nineteenth century. Both Pre-Raphaelites, and born just a year apart, they worked closely together before founding the decorative arts firm Morris, Marshall, Faulkner and Co. in 1861. I loved Morris glass, though I'd not come across that much. Actually, I had, and it was about to bear fruit; I just didn't know it at the time.

I was in the workshop with Darren working on some pieces when a call came in on my brand-new mobile phone from a dealer who was making a fortune shipping stuff to the United States. He told me he had a load of stained-glass windows he'd come across and wanted to move them on.

I told him to bring them over so I could have a look. A couple of hours later he showed up, and when he opened the back of his van I just stood there trying not to gawp.

'Where did you get this?' I asked.

'Demolition contractor. He died recently and his wife called me to clear the house. Do you want it or not?'

For a moment I didn't speak. What I was looking at was the same stack of windows we'd removed from the Holyhead church on my second day working with Gordon Stewart. That was the day after I unloaded Michael Maine's van and knew this was exactly what I wanted to do. That was also the day I learned how to remove the glass without damaging it. The same batch of windows the contractor had wanted to keep, he'd done nothing with them, and now they were back with me.

It had been eight years since I'd seen them and a few pieces were in much better condition than the others. Taking my time, I turned back a couple to have a closer look and heard a sharp intake of breath. Glancing over my shoulder I could see Darren with his mouth hanging open.

'Don't say a word,' I whispered.

Three of the pieces were William Morris. When I'd painstakingly removed them from that old church, I knew nothing about him, but I did now. I could feel the hairs prickle on the back of my neck.

'What d'you want for it?' I said to the dealer, trying to sound as deadpan as I could.

'Four grand.'

I made a face. 'I've got three and a bit in cash.'

'Alright,' he said. 'That'll do.'

It was incredible, one of those moments that's unlikely ever to be repeated. Even now, when I think about it, I have to pinch myself. The dealer had no idea of their real worth and neither did I. But I had a hunch, and as soon as he'd gone I picked up the phone to a guy called Neil Phillips I'd met at Newark. In those days he was the biggest dealer of stained glass in the world; his family owned Hardman & Co., an incredibly successful manufacturer who started making Gothic stained-glass windows in the nineteenth century at the suggestion of Augustus Pugin, the architect who designed the Palace of Westminster.

I spoke to Neil and told him what I had and he said he wanted to see it. He wasn't going to drive all the way to Conwy, though, so I fetched my dad's knackered old Nikon and took photos of the three Morris windows, using the backdrop of my mum's kitchen window so you could see them properly. Film in hand, I trotted down to Boots, put it in to be developed and picked up the photos the next day. I sent them off and first thing the following morning Neil was on the phone.

'What d'you want for them?' he said.

I really didn't know, but one was called 'Voyage to Vinland the Good' and it was a belter.

'A lot,' I said. 'I know what I've got.'

'OK. Bring them down so I can see.'

'Can I come now?'

'Fine. I'll be waiting for you.'

After putting down the phone, I jumped in my van (by now a slightly less-shit Mercedes 208) and drove to Birmingham to show the windows to Neil. 'Voyage to Vinland' was actually by Morris & Co., which meant it was manufactured after William Morris's death, but it had been designed by him, Dante Gabriel Rossetti and Burne-Jones in period. I had done a bit more research and discovered that they'd only manufactured three. One had disappeared, one was in a museum in New York and the other belonged to me.

As soon as I got to Neil's place, I opened the back of the van and unwrapped the cloths. I could see his reaction, though, being a savvy guy, he did his best not to let it show.

I waited while he took a closer look.

'What do you think?' I said after he'd had a moment to evaluate what he was looking at.

He didn't reply and that's always a good sign. If something is crap people are very quick to let you know. I didn't press him. I knew what I had, so I waited.

'Alright,' he said. 'I'll give you fifty thousand for the three.'

I could feel the hairs again on the back of my neck. That kind of money was way more than I'd expected and it would have a radical impact on my business. I'd paid just over three grand for the whole lot and he was offering £50,000 for just a few. I should have taken that and shook his hand there and then, but for some reason I didn't.

'It's not enough,' I said, the words just coming out of their own accord; for the life of me I don't know why I said it.

Neil looked at me with a shake of his head and a sharp intake of breath. Then he was quiet for a moment. 'I'll give you fifty-five,' he said, 'but you have to leave them with me.'

I held out my hand and we shook on it.

'You can have them when the cheque clears,' I said.

That kind of find is something you never forget and it allowed me to pump money into stock so I could begin to expand the business. Looking back now it shows me how much I'd learned in a relatively short space of time and how ballsy I could be when it came to negotiation. Some 25 years later, both those skills were called for as the chilly spring of 2019 became a decent summer. At times it was absolutely blistering. Take 25 July, for example, not just the second hottest day of the year, it was close to the all-time record. Temperatures were supposed to hit more than 38°C and that was going to be painful. According to the news the roads would melt, power lines might sink and the train tracks were likely to buckle, so the trains would have to run at half-speed. It was hotter than it had been in Italy where I'd spent the last ten days trying to have a bit of a holiday while tracking down as much fresh stock as I could carry in my suitcase. I don't mind relaxing by the pool and it's important to recharge the batteries, but Italy is the country that brought us the Renaissance and there's always something that catches my eye. You don't have to go looking for it either, not with so many galleries and junkshops, not to mention stands selling stuff by the side of the road. Before my girlfriend Sam and I left for home, I'd bought 46 prints that I'd stripped from their frames and rolled up so I could get them in my suitcase. They weren't classic in terms of art, but they all had something about them. I've got an art-critic friend who jokingly likes to tell me that I have no taste, but he's not looking at the paintings the way I do. We don't buy for the same reason – to an art critic it's about the painting itself whereas to me it's the decorative quality. By that I mean how it speaks to me, how it's going to look hanging on the wall, so the subject matter or the artist, its place in the history of art, is less important.

Italy has to be my favourite country; I love the architecture and art, the food, the people and the relaxed way of living that's echoed in the quality of the wine. Many really good reds come from Italy, not least Valpolicella Ripasso, which I discovered on my third or fourth Decorative Fair at Battersea. That event holds huge importance for me and for all sorts of reasons. It's the most important date in the calendar and not just in terms of where an antique dealer is able to exhibit. It's only for dealers at the top of their game in terms of the quality of stock they deal in. You have to apply, and you're vetted before you're admitted.

On the day I discovered my love of Valpolicella Ripasso, I'd been at the fair for a couple of days and had arranged to deliver an Empire cellarette to a client on Cheyne Walk. A cellarette is a smallish wooden cabinet or box, which comes in a variety of different styles and designs, that was used to cool wine bottles at lavish parties. It was a piece I'd wanted to shift for a while and we'd been using it throughout the day to store open bottles of wine which we'd share with customers and other dealers. That's the nature of Battersea, it's not just about the quality of the antiques, it's about the people that get to display there: it's a very special place to be.

I remember being on my stand around lunchtime when this lairy, slightly scary-looking guy kept walking past and seemed to know everybody I did. At least six-foot-four, his name was Rob Black, a dealer I knew by reputation with an 'in-your-face' look about him. The third time he walked by, he spoke to me.

'Drew,' he said. 'I've been hearing good things about you. I like the cut of your jib. We should talk. How d'you fancy having dinner later?'

'Alright. I'll be finished around six.'

He showed up about quarter past and I was trying to work out how I was going to get the cellarette to Cheyne Walk.

'Alright, Drew,' he said, in an accent reminiscent of Del Boy in *Only Fools and Horses*. 'Are we set?'

'Pretty much, but I've sold this piece and I have to deliver it before we go.'

He recognised the cellarette as the one we'd used to store the bottles of wine we'd been drinking throughout the day. It was about 130cm long and 75cm tall, a bit of a beast with Empire feet, and I was glad to be rid of it. Empire is an early nineteenth-century design style that originated in France and was named after the Emperor Napoleon. An obvious example is the Arc de Triomphe that was commissioned after the Battle of Austerlitz during the Napoleonic Wars. Square, solid and functional, the cellarette echoed that style and would've been used at parties in rich people's houses. Packed with ice to keep the bottles cool, the residue drained from a plug in the base when the party was over.

'I tell you what,' he said. 'I'll give you a hand to carry it outside. We'll chuck it in a cab and drop it off then you can buy me dinner after.'

I seemed to remember him inviting me to dinner, but it really didn't matter who was paying, because I'd had a terrific day. Between us we manhandled the cellarette out to the street where we hailed a cab and drove to this fantastic townhouse on Cheyne Walk. Most of the adjoining properties had long since been turned into apartments but my client still owned his entire building. He told us he'd bought it in 1960 for pennies and now it was worth a fortune.

'What do you do again?' I asked him.

'I'm an estate agent. Land agent, actually, I do a lot of work for the Prince of Wales.'

We carried the cellarette inside and there was Empire furniture everywhere. Big stuff and lots of it; really over-the-top. To tell you the truth, Rob and I were a little tipsy so it was more of a chore than it should've been. The task was made harder when the guy said he wanted the cellarette on the top floor, but up we went with Rob cracking jokes about holding his end up and the agent joining in with the banter. Finally, we negotiated all four flights of stairs and, as we put the cellarette down, I glanced over my shoulder. I went very cold, suddenly completely sober. All the way down the stairs, and I'm talking all four flights, were splashes of red wine, made all the more obvious by the snow-white Axminster carpet.

'Oh shit,' I said, as the owner of the house looked where I did. We'd been stacking those open bottles all day and some of the wine must've spilled out into the bottom of the cellarette and seeped through the plug as we tilted it when we were climbing. I could not believe what I was seeing: instead of a profit, I was looking at a £20,000 bill for re-carpeting.

'God,' I said. 'I'm so sorry. I don't know what to say. I really am so sorry, believe me.'

Even Rob was aghast, but the owner just shook his head and reached in his pocket for his wallet. 'Don't worry about it,' he said. 'It's nothing that can't be fixed.' God bless him, he gave us a 50-quid tip.

I couldn't believe his reaction. He said the insurance would pay, it was one of those things and he genuinely wasn't concerned about it. Outside we hailed another cab and Rob gave the driver directions to take us to what turned out to be the best Italian restaurant I'd ever been to. He told me not to tell anyone because the place was the best-kept secret in London and he wanted it to remain that way. As we walked in the owner approached us with a welcoming smile. 'Boys,' he said, 'you look tired. Sit down and I will feed you like you've never been fed before.' We sat down at a table in the back and I took a look at the menu.

'Can I bring you a glass of wine?' the owner asked us.

'Thanks.' I needed a drink, having barely recovered from the episode with the carpet. 'That would be wonderful.'

A couple of minutes later he was back with two glasses of the best red wine I'd ever tasted. I knew about Valpolicella, of course, but I'd not drunk the Ripasso. It was really, really good; so good that, when the food came, I asked the waiter to bring us a bottle. Rob likes a drink. I mean he really likes a drink, and I've been known to sink a few myself, but back then I had no idea what kind of long-term effect that was going to have and how it would bite me later. By the time they brought the risotto we'd already drunk most of it, so I ordered another bottle. I'm a fan of risotto but this was like nothing I'd ever tasted. It arrived on a chunk of Parmesan cheese that had to be 45cm tall with a triangle cut out of the top. The risotto had been layered inside so, when the waiter served, he scooped out not only risotto but softened Parmesan cheese as well. It was the best Italian meal I've ever had and we quickly polished off the second bottle of Ripasso. I asked the waiter to bring another and we drank that, so I told him to keep it coming until we could barely raise our lips from the table. When the bill arrived, I found that the wine alone was £130 a throw. I didn't care. I'd avoided a £20,000 bill for four flights of Axminster stair carpet.

CHAPTER 3

FROM THE
GROUND UP

So, 25 July 2019 was the second hottest day of the year, and I was only just back from the holiday/buying trip to Italy. It was Thursday and I was driving the short distance to the warehouse at Colwyn Bay to check on a batch of furniture the lads had brought back from Carmarthen in the early hours of the morning. Just a couple of miles from where I live in Conwy, the warehouse is small and compact, occupying one corner of a cul-de-sac of terraced houses. I rent it from Craig Hughes, who does all the reupholstery for me, and his place is on the other corner. The road in is pretty tight, always packed with cars, but there's just enough room to reverse a Luton up to the warehouse gates.

Before I left, I opened all the doors in my house then followed Enzo out to where the grass needed cutting badly. I like things a little wild, but this was ridiculous, and he'd need a snorkel if he was going to check out who'd been in his garden. As luck would have it, a lad was working on a neighbour's place across the road so I asked him if he could look at mine and he said he'd mow the lawn for me later.

I had to leave Enzo lying on the cool slate floor, which was his favourite spot, because it was too hot for him to be in the car. I left every window in the house open, which made it cool enough, and I gave him a chew (which is a slice of heaven to a Jack Russell) before leaving for the warehouse. More than a year had passed since I'd agreed to buy the furniture and I couldn't remember much of it. But I don't buy crap so, hopefully, the return would be worth the wait.

In one of those weird sets of circumstances that can happen in this trade, it began with a phone call from a guy who told me he was a property developer and antique dealer.

'Look,' he said. 'I've bought this old office in Carmarthen that's been used by at least four or five generations of solicitors and there's a whole stack of furniture.' That was odd because generally dealers don't ask for properties to be cleared, we're the ones doing the clearing.

'Do you want to come down?' he asked me.

'I don't know,' I said. 'Depends what's in there. Can you send me a couple of pictures?'

Carmarthen is a four-hour drive from Conwy and I didn't want to make the trip without some idea of what I'd be looking at. The market for 'Industrial Furniture' is generally good, though, and I've managed to do pretty well from it over the years. If this bloke wasn't bullshitting, it might have something going on. Five generations meant the stuff should be at least a hundred years old, maybe a hundred and fifty.

Later that day the pictures came through and, from what I could see, the place looked as if it was worth a visit, but when I spoke to him again the developer told me that time was tight and he only had a couple of hours he could spare, so we had to make a firm arrangement. Once again, I wondered if this guy was telling the truth because, if he'd bought the place, then time shouldn't be such a problem. On the other hand, if the sale wasn't complete and all he had were the keys, he'd have to make sure he got them back to the agent pretty sharpish.

By the time I left I was more than a little suspicious but made the journey anyway. It took the full four hours before I arrived in a tiny Carmarthenshire village where the buildings slumped so much it looked as though the place had melted. It wasn't easy to access either; the roads were so narrow it was a struggle to get my four-by-four through without scratching the paintwork to pieces. A maze of tight little streets with nowhere to park; in the end I dumped the car, knowing I would come back to a parking ticket.

Finally, I found the building and it was a huge Georgian affair that towered over the street. I was beginning to think that, despite my suspicions, this call might have some potential. I was a bit late and the developer was looking at his watch, literally hopping from one foot to the other. He was agitated and certainly pressed for time and I knew then he hadn't bought the building. When it came to opening the door, he was fumbling around trying to find the right key and I realised I was here so he could use my expertise to find out what extra value there might be inside that he could weigh against the price he was paying.

It didn't matter; there might be a deal here so long as he was in a position to buy and not just a wannabe. Finally, he got the door open and it was worth the wait because I found myself walking into Ebenezer Scrooge's office. It was dark and cool, shadows in every corner, with four or five floors accessed by an ancient winding staircase. The steps were incredibly worn, broken in places and repaired with bits of old tin; I imagined Bob Cratchit going up and down by the light of a candle.

The first thing that caught my eye was a pair of tall oak bookcases. I didn't say anything and the guy showed me another two that were slightly smaller but, in many ways, just as impressive as the first. As we went deeper into the building, I came across another pair, the largest bookcases I'd ever seen in fact, and that really set the juices flowing. Fixed to both wall and floor, they towered all the way to the ceiling and I reckoned they'd be a bitch to get out but, hopefully, the lads would be able to do it.

'Impressive,' I said. 'So, what's for sale?'

'All of it.' He gestured. 'For the right price you can clear it.'

I moved from room to room and there were lots of bits and pieces, some of which I knew I could move pretty quickly. I picked out an old clerk's stool where the seat was worn at the front to the point it was sloping. The foot rail was bowed and worn, which indicated decades of use where some poor guy with a pen and parchment had worked away at his ledgers. I wondered how many clerks had sat on that stool. I thought about all the people who had worked in this place poring over contracts and documents.

There was something going on in every room and that included an attic full of solicitor's deed boxes. You know the kind of thing; large, made of metal, with the names of each estate written on them. The roof had been leaking, the place stank of damp and some of the boxes had popped open. Everywhere I looked there were papers; loads of them, literally tens of thousands of documents and all hand-written. The attic was split into two separate rooms, but I could barely get the door that separated them open. Weighing in with my shoulder, I managed to get it cracked far enough to stick my head around and saw it was crammed full of metal shelves and more deed boxes. Back when this was a working practice they would have been taken into court and various documents used as evidence. When the case was over, they'd be locked away and returned to the solicitor's office.

'Alright,' I said to the developer. 'I think we can do something. How much do you want for it?'

'Fifteen grand.'

That wasn't going to happen, 15 was way too steep. I had to bring this guy down to earth. 'I can't do that,' I said. 'I'll give you four thousand.'

He was shaking his head. 'I can't do four, not for all of it.'

'Alright,' I said. 'Let me look around some more and have a think.'

The guy was checking his watch, but he left me to have a wander so I totted up what it would cost to hire a couple of vans, pay for the diesel and wages of the boys that would come down here and collect it. There was a lot of work to be done and the tallest bookcases would be tough to get out and, on that second look, I decided half of the stuff wouldn't be worth the trouble anyway.

'I tell you what I'll do,' I said when I went back to him. 'I'll cherry-pick the bits I really want and leave you with the majority.'

'For four grand?'

'Five,' I said. 'That's the best I can do.'

He took a moment to think, then, begrudgingly, he shook hands with me.

I left him to contact me with a date when we could come down and headed back to my parking ticket. I was right about him not being a dealer and I was right about the state of play as regards the building. He was in the market for sure, but I soon discovered just how far he was from actually owning the place. We'd shaken hands on a deal for some of the contents but I didn't hear anything for over a year. I'd almost forgotten in fact when, finally, he called me.

'Right,' he said. 'The building is mine. Can you come and clear it right away?'

I had to think about that because we get calls about clearances on a daily basis and the diary is booked out for weeks.

'Can't do it for a month,' I said. 'We're pretty tied up and it's been a year since you talked to me.'

He wasn't happy but there was nothing I could do about that; if he wanted us, he had to accept our schedule. He'd kept me waiting a year so another month wouldn't hurt, though it was more like six weeks before the boys were able to make it.

It was 24 July when four guys drove down in two vans led by my full-time restorer Gavin and another good lad called Elwyn. They left Conwy at half-five in the morning and, around lunchtime, I'd had a phone call.

'Drew, it's Gav. We've got a problem.'

'What's up?'

'The two biggest bookcases, those massive ones attached to the wall – we can't get them free without tearing everything up and, even if we could, we'll never get them out the door.'

Shit, I thought. I'd been looking forward to getting those back. I knew they'd be a bitch but I hadn't known it would be this bad. Gavin's been with me for 20 years, though, and if he says he can't get something out of a building, it can't be done. When we met, he was about to start playing professional football in Florida but a snapped Achilles tendon put an end to his career before it ever began. He had to come back to Wales and, if you ask him where we met, he'll look you in the eye and tell you – deadpan – it was a gay bar, but really it was a farm shed. His mum and dad were cleaning the farmhouse I was living in at the time, and I needed someone to clear out a shed. They roped Gav in to help, and he and I got talking about the restoration business. He was keen to learn so I gave him a job and he's been with me ever since. I like to keep things local: most of the people I work with go back to the days when we kicked a ball about or climbed the scrapyard fence and tried to avoid the Alsatians.

Gavin can spot the value in a broken-down item and loves the fact he's on a constant learning curve. The job isn't without its risks; he still carries the scars from the time he nearly lost his arm to a stained-glass window. About 15 years ago, we were stripping out a local school with the same Gordon Stewart who gave me my apprenticeship. There was a lot to do and Gavin said he was going to climb a ladder and take out the upper window.

'Not on your own, mate,' I told him.

'It's fine. I'll be OK.'

'Gavin,' I said, 'there's no way you can take that window out by yourself, you need someone to foot the ladder.' I told him to wait for Gordon because the floor of the school hall had been polished to the point it was slick. But Gavin wasn't going to wait for anyone: he shimmied up the ladder and, of course, the feet slipped and he went straight through the window we were supposed to be removing. He hit the ground with blood spurting from a massive wound that all but sliced his arm off. We had to rush him to hospital, where a plastic surgeon had to reattach the blood vessels before they could stitch him up; he could barely move it for weeks after.

I had to suck up the loss of the big bookcases, but I wasn't going to part with five grand if it didn't include the two best pieces. There was some renegotiating to do, so I spoke to the developer and we did a little bit of back and forth before I ended up knocking 1,500 quid off the total. We were down to £3,500 now, but I spoke to Gavin again and he told me about another bookcase he'd spotted that he thought was worth a punt. He's got a good eye and I trust him so I bought that for £400. With a final tally of £3,900, they loaded up the vans and set out on the long drive home.

As I pulled up outside the warehouse, they were already unloading. After finding somewhere to park, I squeezed past the van and found Gavin in the yard with sweat rolling off him in rivers. It was baking in the yard, way hotter than it had been in Italy.

'You found the place then?' I said.

He muttered something about narrow fucking streets in the middle of fucking nowhere then rolled a cigarette. 'Pity about those bookcases. There's some good stuff here, but those were the jewels, weren't they?'

'You really couldn't get them out?'

'Not without taking out a bay window, and the building's listed.'

'So what? You can take the window out and put it back after. What is it – four screws and a bit of cement?'

'Tell that to the developer.'

Gav disappeared inside the warehouse as the other lads manhandled the larger bookcase over. Moments later the front doors opened, exposing the upper floor where Gav had the hoist ready. As they hauled the bookcase up, I could see it needed a little work on a cornice, so I made a mental note to phone Kevin, or 'Mr Measures', the guy I turn to for really intricate woodwork. The other bookcases were in good order, just a case of putting the shelves back and rubbing down with a cloth. By the end of the day they'd be photographed and on display in the showroom.

I followed Gav inside and he drew my attention to a chest of drawers I'd bought from Sir James Shuckburgh of Shuckburgh Hall in Northamptonshire. It had been in a hell of a state when we found it, but Kevin had been working on it and he'd done a shit-hot job as always. Precise, meticulous: 'Measures' by name and measures by nature; we couldn't have come up with a better nickname. Up here everyone has one: there's T, of course, and Daz-Babs. There's a lad we call Johnny-Five because, if you tell him something, five minutes later he's forgotten. I've got a mate called 'Phil the Box' who's a funeral director and the best of all is Dave Tuesday. Me and T were sitting in the pub one night having a pint when this really big bloke walked in and the whole room seemed to part like a wave before him.

'Who's that?' I asked as he strode past our table.

'Dave Tuesday,' T said.

'Why'd they call him that?'

'Because if he says it's Tuesday – it's fucking Tuesday.'

I called Mr Measures and told him I loved what he'd done with the chest; the only thing he still had to do was a bit of 'cock-beading'. That's a narrow, semi-circular bead which is slightly pronounced and quite often appears as decoration on drawers and doors of this age. Even Gav was impressed with the quality: the chest had been derelict when we dragged it out, but now it looked fantastic. The best restoration is when a piece is brought back to the condition it should be in given its age, without looking like it had been anywhere near an expert. With this piece, two of the handles had been missing, the legs were rotten and the sides bashed in. Looking at it now, I couldn't tell which were the old handles and which were the ones Kevin had made to replace them. The chest had been made by a provincial country manufacturer around 1825 and it was painted with faux-marbling. That was a common practice back then and

I like that sort of naivety. It's attractive and it makes an item look much more expensive than it was back then. I think I paid about 250 quid for this one and had another 250 in it. Now it was restored we should see 850 and someone would be very happy to pay it. It's not a massive profit, what we call a 'turn', and most of the time that's all there is. The big-ticket stuff is sporadic but it's out there and when you come across it there's money to be made, as I found out with those William Morris panels.

Satisfied we'd see a decent enough return, I took a look around the workshop to check on a few other items we'd yet to get to. Against the far wall was a pair of large desks I'd bought in Belgium, an old nineteenth-century haberdashery cabinet that needed a new side, and some stuff Gav clearly didn't want to be bothered with because he'd hidden it right at the back of the workshop. One thing caught my eye, the industrial table I'd bought in Chorley. It hadn't been photographed yet because Gav was using it as his workbench.

With photographs in mind, I took another look at the larger bookcases. They were really very handsome, with a plaque on each that confirmed they'd been presented to a vicar in Swansea in 1909. That was important, no guesswork here, we had provenance, the year they were made, and that added to the value. They were high quality, constructed from oak (though the backboards were pine, which lessened the value fractionally). Solid oak brings the most money, but these had adjustable shelving and the original dust-falls (removable leather flaps) that fit between the underside of the shelf and the top of the books to keep the dust off.

'What do you reckon we should ask for them?' I said to Gav.

'Twenty-eight hundred.'

'I was thinking two-seven so we're not far apart. Alright, two-eight.' I asked him to get them to Eleri (our brilliant photographer) as soon as possible.

Gavin showed me the bookcase he'd told me about on the phone that was complete with a set of solicitor's deed boxes. The lads lifted it out of the van and I took a look at the labelling: SEQUESTRATION OR DEBT ENFORCEMENT.

'You don't want to be on the end of that,' I said to nobody in particular.

Gav was standing next to me. 'My name'll be in there somewhere. CCJ behind it.'

The bookcase itself wasn't in the best of condition. At one time it had a set of doors but they'd been ripped off and that had caused the wood to crack down one side. It's the kind of thing that really grates on me.

'Why would anyone do that?' I said. 'Three screws; all you have to do is take them out. Why rip the bloody doors off?'

It was a shame because it was so unnecessary, but we weren't going to make another set – it wouldn't be cost-effective. Instead, Gav would splice some wood into the groove where the hinges had been and bead over the top. He'd match the colour with wax and it would go straight onto the website as a set of open pigeonholes.

For me this is the most exciting aspect of the job. Buying is great, but restoration is where I started, and I never get tired of breathing new life into something that's been left to rot. The lads were already on it and, this afternoon, we'd have the bookcases with Eleri, who would take the photos. They'd be on display in the showroom and this evening I would put them on the website. That's how quick we can work without cutting any corners in the restoration process. We make money, sometimes lots of it, and we get the odd derogatory tweet … but there's a cost nobody sees. It's not just the difference between what we pay for something and what we sell it for; it's four lads, two vans, warehousing, the shop and website, as well as the cost of the restoration before it gets anywhere near a professional photographer.

Adding stuff we've bought and restored to the website is a huge part of what we do. It's a job only I do, and I'm meticulous about freshening the inventory. We sell a lot through the shop, it's important to have a physical presence, but the sales are nothing compared to the website.

When I first realised its potential, it was another 'Eureka' moment, probably the most important discovery I've ever made. Even now, not all dealers have a decent web presence, but when I realised there was a way of reaching the entire planet, 20 years ago, I jumped right on it. I went to see a mate called Rob Wilding from Ruthin, when I was working every second of every day but there were only so many deals to be made by physical contact or a phone call. I was frustrated, thinking that there had to be more to the business than grinding myself into the dust trying to see as many customers as possible. I knew Rob was making a small fortune selling car parts online, but had no idea what that was. He was into old cars and had discovered a niche bringing old VWs in from California to break down and sell as spares. I called by his place to get some parts for my Beetle and discovered he'd made enough money to buy a house, garage and storage shed.

I was like, 'Mate, how're you doing this?'

'Internet.'

'What's the internet?' (Yes, I really did say that. I hadn't got a clue.)

'The worldwide web.'

'What?'

'I've got a website.' He told me how he was using his computer to sell the parts he'd broken to customers all over the country. He showed me the website, and I could feel a tremendous sense of excitement. That's it, I thought, that's how I'm going to do it. That's how I can bring what I do to everyone and not just in this country. The antiques trade knows no boundaries. If I did this right, I could sell all over the world.

I spoke to a couple of people and within four weeks I had a computer, a website and a database. From that moment on I started selling stuff and in the next six weeks I'd turned over more than I'd done the entire previous year. It was like being back at Newark only tenfold and the whole world was my oyster. I sold to one of the Spice Girls. I sold to Diane Keaton and Marco Pierre White. I was all over the salvage news; the website had changed my world completely.

Gav was making a start on the clerk's stool where a few dots of white paint mottled one leg. He'd leave that; if the whole thing was coated, he'd rub it down, but those dots were part of the stool's story. By the end of the day the work would be done and it would join the bookcases in the photo studio. Sometimes it's that simple and with others it's complicated, like the chest of drawers from Shuckburgh. Either way, we're particular about how we restore things. Everything Gav was doing right now he'd learned from me and I'd learned it from Gordon Stewart and Joe Sturges during my apprenticeship in Abergele. It's a tradition that demands a lot of hard work and commitment, not to mention knowledge that can only be gained from experience. Gordon passed on what he knew to me, like a father figure; he helped me become the restorer I am today.

Since then I've been involved in replacing windows at Conwy Castle, and recreating Hogwarts School for a

Japanese businessman. I've done work for Disney and, a few years ago, I rebuilt the oldest stained-glass window in Wales at a church in Holt near Wrexham. I remember the first day on the job we were working on what's called a 'medley window'. During the Reformation, when Henry VIII was raiding the monasteries, a lot of windows were taken out and buried to stop them being destroyed. Much of it got smashed, though, and had to be pieced together in medley windows after it had been dug up again. The one we worked on had been inscribed by the man who put it back together in the eighteenth century; a lovely find that set the tone for the rest of the project.

I love old churches, they're a massive part of my life but not for religious reasons, as I'm a committed atheist. Ever since I can remember, I've wanted to own one, and I got my chance at 24 when I was still working out of those two rooms under my dad's workshop. It was ridiculous really, the ceiling was so low I scraped the top of my head, and I'm not the tallest guy in the world. But it didn't cost much and the money I was making was going back into the business.

I'm told I have an artistic eye and I probably get it from my father. I mentioned before that we have a shit relationship now, but when I first started to show an interest in antiques, he was actually pretty supportive. When I was only about eight or nine, I remember going shopping with my mum to help her pick out the clothes she wanted to buy. I would tell her what colours and style suited her, and my dad must've picked up on it because initially he tried to help me develop that eye. He's an incredibly talented artist, not just with paint, but sculpture and music. In the early 1950s he contracted tuberculosis and was sent to an isolation hospital where he had a lot of time to paint. TB was a killer back then; he told me that the closer your bed was to the door the sicker you knew you were, because there would be less disturbance to the other patients if you died in the night. When he got better, he went to work for a sign-writer in Llandudno, a lovely man called Mr Traversie, who helped bring on his talent.

Aware I had a similar appreciation for form and colour, he'd show me different paintings and ask what I thought was wrong with them. Invariably, I would pick up on something: a horse for example; the way a hoof was set, I'd want it at a slightly different angle. I was still only eight or nine, but he'd take me to stand in front of a building somewhere and ask me to tell him what I could see. Again, I would pick up on details: a window or beam, the thickness of a wall mounting or windowsill. Buildings, cars, art: I had a critical eye, one that could see beauty and potential where others couldn't.

Art was really important to my dad and, whenever he managed to scrape a little bit of money together, he would take me and my younger brother Guy to a museum. He would sit us in front of masterpieces and ask what we thought of them. Guy wasn't quite as interested as I was. We were pretty close as kids, but he chose a completely different career path to me. I loved being in those museums and still do. I didn't know anything about art. I didn't know the names of any of the artists, but I didn't care; there was beauty here and I appreciated it.

Ever since Dad first stood me in front of those old buildings, I've had a thing for Georgian architecture, particularly the British Regency period. In 1811 the mad King George III had been deemed unfit to rule and his son was named Prince Regent. There was a particular style about the buildings they built between then and 1820 that I don't think has been bettered. John Nash was one of the leading architects of the time and did some amazing things up and down the country. Regency is about proportion and space, ceiling height and window arrangement, or 'fenestration' as it's referred to. Most of the Georgian buildings had windows that graduated in size, which gave the façades a fantastic aesthetic. Bath is probably the best example, along with sections of Edinburgh, and there are large swathes, of course, in London.

Anyway, I was in the workshop one day when a friend of mine called on my mobile phone. 'Drew, it's Andy. I was wondering if I could borrow your van?'

'Of course. What d'you want it for?'

'Andrea has to move out of her house and I said I'd give her a hand.'

CHAPTER 3

Andrea was Andy's sister so I told him I'd help with the move and asked where she lived.

'A knackered old church house,' he said, 'in the Conwy Valley.'

I picked him up and he directed me through Eglwys-bach to a beautifully tranquil spot made all the more so by a Regency Methodist chapel. It was the most amazing location and, as we drove up the overgrown lane, the hairs started to climb on the back of my neck. There were three buildings, including a two-storey stable block, a church house and the chapel itself, which was pretty much derelict. Andrea came out to meet us and I asked her why she was moving.

'I have to,' she said. 'They've sold the place.'

I took a closer look at the chapel and it was exactly the sort of building I'd dreamed of owning. The windows were wonderful, there was space and light, and the location was pure magic. As we started loading her gear into the van, I asked if she had any idea how much the seller had been asking, but all she could tell me was that someone had bought it and she had to vacate. I was intrigued now and wondered what the exact position was, because something is only ever 'sold' (and therefore out of reach) if money has changed hands. Right then I didn't know if that was the case or not, so I decided to do some digging.

Before we left, I wandered through a forest of two-metre-tall bracken that surrounded the chapel and could see where the roof had fallen in completely. There was no running water or inside toilet. Peeking through a window, I could tell that the floors were slate laid straight onto dirt – this place was totally virgin. The roof of the two-storey stable block was on the floor and the church house was very basic. Nothing had been touched since the place had been abandoned by the Methodists and I was determined to buy it.

Back in Conwy I rang the estate agent and asked him what was going on.

'Oh yeah, that place. It's sold,' he said. 'There's no point looking at it.'

'OK, I understand. Can I talk to the person who sold it?'

'No, you can't. The deal's already done, it's all taken care of.'

'Has money changed hands, contracts exchanged? When's completion?'

He couldn't tell me; he was mumbling, fumbling, and that aroused my suspicions. I was sure no deal had been completed, but when I pressed him, he refused to give me any details. I didn't leave it there. I made a right old noise, calling every council in North Wales, trying to find out who the seller was and who was planning to buy it. Word got back to the estate agent and we had another conversation.

'Look,' he said. 'The fact is, it isn't "sold" sold yet, but …'

'Well, if it's not sold, I want to buy it.'

CHAPTER 3

'You can't, somebody else is. It's not available.'

Bullshit. If something's for sale and no money's changed hands then it's still available. I put down the phone, then rang the Royal Commission for Wales who note the cultural importance for all such buildings.

'Oh,' they said. 'That one. It's been going on for a very long time and, as far as we know, nothing has been completed.' They told me a sale had been agreed for £17,000 but no contracts had been exchanged. I did some more digging and it turned out the place had never been on the open market. We're talking about an acre of land, a chapel and house, as well as a two-storey stable block, and the price was just £17,000.

I got back on the phone to the agent and told him I knew the chapel had never reached the open market. Legally, an agent has to put a property on the open market and it seemed he'd been keeping this place back so a mate of his could buy it. Now he had no choice and it would go to sealed bids. I was determined to get it, so I called Richard, another estate agent I knew.

'How much do you think this place is going to cost me if I want to secure it?' I asked.

'I'll find out.' He hung up and ten minutes later he phoned back. 'Go in at £31,500,' he said.

I did that, wrote my bid and sealed the envelope, then drove to the estate agent and stuffed it through the letterbox. Nine o'clock the next morning I called to ask if my bid had won and they said they'd phone back in an hour and let me know. That hour came and went and nobody phoned. The day dragged on and still the phone didn't ring. I was beginning to wonder if the figure Richard had given me was too low, then, right at the end of the day, the agents finally rang me. 'It's yours,' they said. 'You won the bid.'

I could not believe it. I was the owner of a Regency building, something I'd dreamed about since I was a kid. I was absolutely euphoric, but I hadn't paid for it yet. I had to get a mortgage, but the place was so bad the agents didn't think anyone would lend on it. I had the deposit, however, and I knew what I was going to do with the place; it was a question of persuasion. When I sat down with the mortgage advisor, I told her a load of old cobblers about how much money I had and how I was going to spend it. What I wanted from her was the means to complete the purchase, but she didn't think it was worth lending on. I didn't let go. I kept on and on, basically chatting her up (which you couldn't do now), and I did have the full deposit. Although she had been pretty sceptical to begin with, it was old-school banking and in the end she agreed, so I got the rest of the money to buy it.

The deal completed on my 25th birthday and I took the day off to celebrate. It was the best present I could've had. I went to pick up the key for the church from the agents but they told me they didn't have one, only for the church house.

'What do you mean, you don't have a key?' I asked them.

'We've never had one. I'm not sure there's ever been one.'

No key then, so what? I'd just have to go up there and break in.

I drove back to the valley and got the door open with a crowbar, having bought the church without ever setting foot inside. Once I was in, I could see just how bad the place really was … we're talking falling to pieces. I didn't give a shit, I knew what I was going to do and, the next day, I took my parents to see it.

'This is it,' I said as I parked in a spot where the bracken didn't swamp everything. 'This is why I needed the mortgage.'

My mum just sat there, staring through the windscreen. 'You borrowed money to buy this? What on earth are you going to do with it?'

'Restore it, look at the position it's in.'

Even she had to agree it was perfect.

'I can build something incredibly special here,' I said. 'The bones of the building are solid; it's all about the location.'

So far, my dad had kept quiet. 'What do you think, Dad?' I asked.

'Fantastic,' he said. 'Brilliant buy. Fantastic.'

Hearing any kind of praise from my father had been rare for a long time, so when he opened his mouth and confirmed what I could see, that was good enough for me. Being an artist, he could see exactly what I did. It wasn't what we were looking at now, it was how it would look when it was finished. But that was a long way off, and for the next four years I immersed myself in the project. During the day I would restore glass, strip doors or sell what I'd bought to the trade at Newark, Manchester and Liverpool. After work I'd drive to the chapel and start tearing the place apart so I could build it backup again. Every scrap of cash I had I'd spend on wages for mates who'd come over to work with me at the weekends. I was pushing ahead with the salvage side of my business, so I was using materials I'd reclaimed to put into the restoration. First it was the chapel house that Andrea had rented, after that the stable block, before I finally got to the chapel itself. I ripped what was left of the house apart, rebuilt from the ground up and, six months after completing the deal, I moved in. I had no back door, just a piece of plywood, and there was no flooring upstairs, only the beams, where I fitted a toilet that rested in full view of everyone on the ground floor. It didn't bother me, but it did bother my girlfriend. She moved in thinking she could help with the restoration only to move out again six days later, and that wouldn't have happened if I'd taken more care of the relationship. But I was obsessed with the work, and it was easier to do that without any distractions, though there were plenty I couldn't have conceived back then that were only just around the corner.

CHAPTER 4

FRIENDS, FURNITURE AND FOUR-WHEELED THINGS OF BEAUTY

With the Carmarthen restoration under way, I left the lads to finish the bookcases and went next door to speak to Craig about some chairs he was working on. He's been around a long time and what he doesn't know about reupholstery isn't worth knowing. A few months back I'd bought this pair of handsome circa-1915 leather armchairs with ball and claw feet, that looked like they'd come from a gentlemen's club somewhere, but needed quite a bit of work before we could sell them. They were missing the cushions and there was a problem with both the front panels sagging way more than they should be. I turned one upside down to get a better look and could see various layers of webbing. 'What happened there?' I asked. 'It looks like it's double-webbed.'

'It is,' Craig said. 'Somebody's gone over it again because a lot of the herring-bone has perished.'

The webbing is there to hold the metal springs in place and that gives the chair its comfort and structure. Craig pointed out what was wrong. 'You see the herring-bone's gone there and there. They've put in jute to support it.'

It didn't look good, something I hadn't noticed when I bought the chairs from a dealer I know in Yorkshire.

'The springs at the front have moved,' Craig went on. 'It's why the whole chair is sagging quite so badly. Problem is, I can't get them back in place without taking the sides off. That's a lot of work but it's the only way to do it.' He paused for a moment then pointed. 'The only other thing to do is try to pack the springs with something.'

I had to think about this because that sounded like a bit of a bodge and we don't bodge any restoration.

'Let's have a look at the other one,' I said, and turned it upside down to find it was in the same condition as the first. 'Craig,' I said. 'My brain says strip them down and do this properly.'

'It's not viable, economically.'

That was a blow because I'd already lost any profit I might've made and was not about to lose more money.

'Look,' he said. 'I can do some packing and it won't be a bodge.' He showed me where he meant to give the springs some support and I knew he would do it properly. 'We can make feather cushions and that'll look really good and both chairs will be good as new.'

'Just a bit of packing?' I said.

'Yeah, here and here.' He indicated.

'Will it last?'

'Of course, if I redo the webbing.' Again, he showed me. 'There might be some small issues with the front edge, but there's nothing we can do about that unless I strip them back completely.'

I took a moment to think, fully aware that if Craig said the repair would last then it would. If the seat still sagged a little at the front, that would be in keeping with the age and wear and was part of the charm I'd seen when I bought them in the first place. I'd paid 900 quid plus shipping, but I'd had them a while and Kevin had already done some work on the ball and claw. I was losing money like a leaking tap and I didn't want to lose any more. 'Do what you can,' I said. 'If I can get close to what I paid for them that'll be something.'

My attention switched to another chair Craig had been working on. Bespoke and semi-circular in design, it had been commissioned for a larger gentleman to kick back in. Its form was perfect and the construction reflected the design of a craftsman named Godwin, but I wanted to do some more research because it could also have been made by Holland & Sons. Either way, I'd bought it a couple of weeks earlier at auction and it needed a massive amount of work to restore correctly so I'd been prepared to pay a maximum of £1,500 plus VAT and commission. As it turned out, when it went under the hammer, I didn't have to pay anything like that. No one outbid my 200 quid and I came away thinking I'd nicked it.

'We'll make the money back here, Craig,' I said. 'Once this is up together, I'm asking six grand, and if it doesn't sell straight away there's a dealer who'll give me four for it.'

So, you win some and you lose some, that's the nature of this business. I had a good feeling about the Holland & Sons chair because there's always a solid market. As I turned to go, I took another envious look at the life-sized elephant head that hangs above the door to Craig's office. It came from the Indian restaurant on the prom in Llandudno and I used to covet it every time I went for a curry. 'You're never going to sell that to me, are you?'

'You know I can't,' he said. 'It's Nicky's.'

Nicky is Craig's wife, who's well known for buying and selling various stuff on the internet. One day a few years ago, a customer came in to check on the reupholster of some dining chairs and asked if Nicky could sell an elephant for him.

'A real one?' Craig said.

'Don't be silly, a model.'

'Sure. Nicky can sell anything.'

The guy went out to his van while Craig went back to work, thinking he was going to bring them a model of some kind. Moments later, the guy was back with another man, hefting the life-sized replica.

Craig stopped what he was doing and gawped. 'What the hell is that?' he demanded.

'It's the elephant I want you to sell for me.'

Nicky, who had been watching from the office, was off her chair and striding across the workshop. 'That's not for sale,' she said in a voice that sounds like chocolate being churned by gravel. 'I'm having it.'

'You what?' Craig said. 'What're you talking about?'

'I'll take it in lieu of the wages you owe me.'

She hadn't been working there long and was yet to be paid, so she took the elephant, which meant Craig had to upholster the dining chairs for nothing.

Having agreed a plan of action on the ball and claw chairs, Craig followed me out to the car. He's a massive petrolhead with both a 1976 Corvette in his shop as well as a 289 small-block Mustang and about forty old motorbikes as well. Given this was the second hottest day of the year I had left the four-by-four at home and was driving my 13-year-old Porsche 911. It's a cabriolet, but with the sun being so hot today I'd not been able to decide whether to have the roof down or use it as a parasol.

'So, you did get it back,' Craig said. 'You told me you found it before you went to Italy.'

I was gazing lovingly at the vehicle. 'I should never have let it go in the first place.'

80

He gestured to the sports exhaust pipes. 'Did you put those on?'

'Yeah, when I owned it the first time.'

I love that car and should never have sold it. A 997 C45 manual in triple black that I bought in 2012 with 18,000 miles on the clock from a woman who'd had it new from the showroom. The 15th 911 I'd owned, but it was the first cabriolet. I kept it for five years and put 50,000 more miles on the clock, because I'm not one of these people who has to have the mileage down to the minimum. People are fixated with low miles but, if the miles are low, you're not driving, and what's the point of a car if not to drive it? 911s will do 250,000 miles on one engine and most of the Porsche mechanics won't touch one that's below 100,000 because it takes that long for the motor to bed in.

For some reason I will never understand, I'd traded this car with a dealer in the Cotswolds for an Aston Martin V8 Vantage. I know Aston Martin make fantastic cars, but this one just didn't do anything for me. I was used to Porsche, Volkswagen and Mercedes and the quality of seamless Teutonic engineering. The way this drove was nothing like that, it felt cheap by comparison and it was just awful. That sounds ridiculous, I know, especially when we're talking about one of the most iconic names in the history of top-end sports car makers. But that's how I felt and, by the time I got home to Conwy, I knew I'd done the wrong thing letting the Porsche go, so I got on the phone to the dealer.

'The 911,' I said. 'I want to buy it back. I can't get on with the Aston Martin.'

'I'm sorry,' he said. 'It's gone already. I had a customer lined up. I've already sold it.'

I was gutted, kicking myself, and spent the next two years trawling the internet for another just like it. I never found one and had almost given up hope until the week before I went to Italy. I was in the shop when one of the girls asked me if I'd mind the till while she went out to get a sandwich. While she was gone, I logged on to the PistonHeads sales hub and typed in my usual search, *Black. Cabriolet. Manual.* The second car that popped up seemed to fit my requirements exactly: a 911 in triple black with sports exhaust and electronic performance chip. When I saw the number plate, I couldn't believe it: YN06 ZDT, my car, the one I'd sold two years previously. It was back with the same dealer, so I sent the guy a text telling him not to sell the car to anyone.

Five days went by with no response and I wasn't really surprised, as I hadn't had much time for the bloke in the first place. Five days to answer a call from someone he knows is good for the money – how do these people ever sell anything? I hadn't found the time to phone him back, as I was up to my neck getting stock we'd restored uploaded to the website. Then, just before I was about to leave for Italy, the dealer was on the phone talking as if I was the best friend he'd lost then found again. I asked if it was my car and he told me nothing had changed save a few more miles on the clock; it was in great condition.

'Right then,' I told him. 'I'll have it.'

What he said next completely changed my opinion of him. He had the car up for a decent price but told me he'd knock three and a half grand off because I'd sold it to him in the first place.

'You're a good customer,' he said. 'And I know you regretted it the moment you traded it. It's yours for what I paid for it.'

That was pretty good of him and I told him I'd pay for it over the phone then send someone down to collect it. I couldn't pick it up myself because I was going away, so Lee Blako went instead. Lee's a good lad I've known a while and he would trailer it back. He duly went down and, the day after I got home from the Italian trip, I woke up to it parked on my drive.

A 911 isn't just a car, it's a rolling work of art. After two long years I was desperate to get behind the wheel, so I took a drive out to see Chris Holt, an old friend who used to work for me. Sadly, he died from motor neurone disease at just 49 years of age and I owed a visit to his grave. He was a huge fan of Porsche and VW, the kind of guy who'd appreciate the story of how I'd sold this car and regretted it every day until I got it back. The last time I saw him was just before he died and, being away filming all the time, I'd neglected him a little. When I saw his dad, he made short work of telling me that his real friends had been there for him and where the hell had I been? It put me off going to the funeral. I wanted to because I'd known Chris and his family since 1986, but his dad seemed so bitter I couldn't bring myself to show up because I didn't want to annoy him any more than I already had. That was in 2017, so I drove to Chris's grave to have a chat with him. Holty, we called him; he was quite a character, with a three-legged cat called Tripod and a house called Holty Towers.

Sitting down beside his grave, I told him I'd got my 911 back. 'You know,' I said, 'the one I regretted selling the moment I drove away in the Vantage.'

Holty knew about my love of cars – Porsche, Volks- wagen and particularly Bugatti. I've owned dozens of VWs and Porsches but never a Bugatti, though I've been in love with them since I first saw the T35. That's one of the most beautiful things a human being has ever created. They came out of the Automobiles Ettore Bugatti factory in Molsheim, a French city in Alsace that had been annexed by Germany in 1871. The factory was founded in 1909. Ettore was Ital- ian by birth, an industrial designer by profession and his brilliance was personified in the detail of his engineering and artistry. His father, Carlo, was also a designer renowned for Art Nouveau furniture and jewellery.

I've owned bits of Bugattis and some very interesting pieces associated with the family but never one of their vehicles. For me the marque marries my love of cars and engineering with my appreciation of great design. If ever anyone got it right, it was Ettore: in every single aspect of everything he did, he just nailed it. He's one of the few designers I've come across who has stuck with me. As I said before, I was taught to appreciate design by my father, who is extremely adept at understanding design. When it's as natural, fluid, brilliant and in balance as it was with Bugatti, it creates an impression that never leaves you. When the T35 came out it was one of the most incredible things on the face of the earth. It was a fast car that won races, but also a masterpiece of design. The very first Monaco Grand Prix was won by an Englishman called William Grover-Williams driving a T35 Bugatti. A larger-than-life character, during the Second World War he was an agent with the Special Operations Executive (SOE) and coordinated a group of undercover operatives that gathered information in France and sent it back to London. A man both incredibly brave and calm, he was caught and executed by the Nazis.

So, when it comes to cars, it's Bugatti and Porsche, closely followed by Volkswagen. It is pronounced *Porsch-a*, by the way: sounds poncey, I know, but that's the correct way to say it.

The first time I saw a Porsche was at Oulton Park when I went to watch a race with my parents. It was the early 1980s and back then everybody parked on the grass verges. Just hovering there as we pulled in was an orange RS 2.7

911. With its big fat Fuchs wheels (first made as 'after-market' accessories for the Porsche 911 in 1965), the grass was brushing the underside of the sills and the car looked like it was floating. I utterly fell for it right there, one of the most beautiful things I'd seen, and that was saying some-thing because my father was driving a Jaguar XK120 he'd restored to mirror the one Humphrey Smith was racing. My father's youth club instructor, Humphrey was a really nice guy who did a bit of private racing in an XK120. It's a stunning-looking car, one of the most beautiful designs ever, only topped when William Lyons cracked out the E-Type. That said, I still think the XK140 coupé in its early variation is one of my top five most beautiful cars of all time along with the Maserati Mistral.

I remember going with my father to buy his XK in Rugeley, Staffordshire. It was a 1950 right-hand drive and had been involved in a big accident that smashed up the side. He paid 1,100 quid for it, and I can't remember who else was with us, but I do remember it was night-time, pour-ing with rain, and we had to load the car onto a trailer. It was partly made of alloy: I think most of them had alloy bonnets, but this one had the bonnet as well as the front wings and boot lid and that made it much rarer. It was a classic even then, but it took my father 15 years to get it restored properly. He did it in Old English white with steel wheels and hubcaps, and, after that, a succession of XKs came through the house, culminating in a 150 drop-top.

The registration number was 9058 HG, in dark blue with blue leather, and had only ever been driven by the chauffeur.

It took me a long time before I was able to buy my first Porsche. I've had over a hundred VWs though. I bought the first one, a camper van, when I was 17 and driving a knackered old yellow Capri called the Flying Banana. A Mark II 1600L, the number plate was KED888P. I'd thrashed it to bits going to and from work in Abergele, so it was long past time for a change when I checked the ads in the paper.

VW SPLIT SCREEN VAN 1967 — £500

I'm having that, I thought, and rang the guy straight away. Three miles as the crow flies, I turned up in my Capri with 150 quid in cash and drove home in my first VW. Back then all my mates had them because they were cool, cheap and fun: you could fix them yourself and there was a big fashion for them. This one was rough as a dog's arse, 1500 single-port engine, and rusted to shit with a clutch that slipped like crazy. I didn't care. I can still remember the smell inside and I fell in love with it; I've not been without a VW since.

It was through the VW scene that I met Clive Holland, who is an extremely good friend and someone I trust implicitly. A couple of years older than me, he had some really cool cars, including the first Cal-look VW in North Wales. It was a style from California, where people had modified

Beetles and notch-back/square-back vans as well as Karmann Ghias with lowered suspension, polished Fuchs and whitewall tyres. It was a fashion thing that Clive latched on to; he was the first guy where we lived to take a really cool car and make it even cooler. I was about 18 at this point and still on the YTS scheme working for Gordon Stewart, but Clive and I decided we could make a few quid on the side if we combined our abilities. He's the kind of guy that can turn his hand to most things and, when he does, he's brilliant, a perfectionist, the most fastidious person I've ever known and especially when it comes to vehicles.

'Drew,' he said one day, 'you've got a knack of finding old cars, haven't you?'

'Yep. Throw me into a village anywhere and I'll do it.'

In those days there were a lot of old cars knocking about so we started driving around to see what we could come up with. We'd pick an area, Llan Ffestiniog for example, and drive up every side road, lane and dead end. What we came across was insane. Over a period, we found two right-hand-drive Type 34 razor-edge Karmann Ghias, and a 21-window right-hand-drive split-screen van. We found a Porsche 914 two-litre, a 356B as well as a 1974 Carrera Targa with a one digit, three-letter number plate and paid only £3,000 for it.

One of the best was a bay-window VW camper van I spotted while I was out and about working with Gordon Stewart. All I clocked was the pop-up roof behind a hedge, but I noted where it was and that weekend me and Clive drove over. We knocked on the door and asked the owner if he was interested in selling. It was a green and white Westfalia conversion, one of the first 1.7-litre fuel-injected models; solid but scruffy, and had clearly been lying for a couple of years. The owner told us it didn't start due to some recurring problem he hadn't been able to fathom. Clive got underneath, rummaged around for no more than 30 seconds then slid out and told me to buy it. I went to see the owner and said that if he had the V5 we'd take the van.

'It doesn't start,' he said. 'How are you going to get it out of here?'

'We'll give it a go,' I said. 'How much do you want for it?'

He took a moment to consider then came back with a figure of 500 quid.

I offered £400, he agreed, so I gave him the cash, signed the V5 and told Clive it was ours now.

'Great,' he said, then slid back underneath and came out another 30 seconds later. He told me it was only the fuel line and all he had to do was reattach it. He got in the cab, turned the key and the van started.

So, I love VWs and I'd righted a wrong with Holty and felt much better for doing it. Over the weekend I got most of the stuff from Carmarthen onto the website and met up with T to go to Cambridgeshire the following Monday.

He asked me how the book was going and I told him I'd managed a couple of chapters.

'Really?' he said. 'That's not bad, the last time we talked you had no idea where to begin.'

'Piccadilly Woods,' I said. 'I took your advice, went up there the other day, but you can't get in. The old fields have been fenced off so there's no way down from the top and you can't get past the houses at the bottom.

'I'll send my drone up,' he said. 'See if anything's down there.' We drove on for a bit, then he said: 'So, is it an autobiography?'

'Partly. I've been writing about the chapel, trying to get across the state it was in when I bought it.'

'Right,' he said. 'If it was a horse, you'd have shot it.'

'Where're we going exactly?' I said. I'd yet to look at the call-sheet.

'Ely, then Duxford. We're at Arabesque Antiques on Thursday.'

That all sounded good, although Arabesque might be a little expensive. It's run by Peter Whipps, a dealer I've known for years who had a stand next to mine in a warehouse emporium in Tetbury, Gloucestershire. Mine's long gone but his is still there, though we were meeting at his warehouse facility in the Midlands.

Ely was the first port of call, however, which involved a long cross-country drive from North Wales. 'Am I in the book?' T asked me.

'Do you want to be?'

'Not really. What's there to say, except we've known each other since we were kids in Glan Conwy?'

'There's plenty to say,' I told him. 'I could tell them your real name or how you're a vegetarian and all you eat is beige porridge wrapped in goat's cheese.'

'You're forgetting the Guinness.'

'Then there's your moniker: The Prince of Darkness.'

'My mum coined that,' he said. 'My superpower was sleep.'

'I remember. We'd roll out of the pub on Friday night and nobody could rouse you until half-time in the football on Saturday.'

We still had some distance to go and soon fell into the kind of comfortable silence born of a 40-year friendship.

I remember first seeing T as I cycled down to the bus stop in Glan Conwy. I was eight years old, riding the Raleigh Chopper I'd wanted for ages. That was the bike to have in 1978 but my parents couldn't afford to get me a new one. Instead my dad found a broken one and between us we took it apart and he resprayed it black – most choppers were orange but black was the colour I wanted. I'd taken the mudguards off, had a whip aerial on the back and only a back brake because I thought front brakes looked stupid. Black is still my thing; designs change and I've moved on from bicycles to cars but it's always been black for me.

CHAPTER 4

The bus stop was where the local kids hung out and one of my mates was talking to another lad riding an orange Raleigh Chopper. He'd just moved from Holyhead to Glan Conwy because his dad was a detective inspector who'd moved to the local station. I liked T immediately. Funny as fuck at eight years old, we hit it off right away. He became part of the gang that I mentioned before, only it had expanded now to include Glyn, Stephen Campbell, as well as Olly, Richard and Peter, and not forgetting Geraint Wellies. We called him that because he always wore welly boots. We were a gaggle of horrible little spotty fuckers who'd go setting fire to things, scrumping apples, letting car tyres down and riding through people's gardens. T was a skinny runt; he only put weight on after drinking too much beer. He was the year above me in school, but we were mates from that day at the bus stop. His surname is Tee, so we lengthened it to Teabag then shortened it to T and that's how he's been known ever since. He's the kind of guy who endears himself to everyone; my mother and grandmother loved him.

I'd like to be able to say we were golden children, but we were right little twats, always trying to get hold of cigarettes and finding dirty mags in hedges. We played at being in the Brixton riots, a bunch of skin-headed mods who were into the second wave of the ska scene with bands like The Specials and Madness. I was so into them; my dad painted the Madness M with Chas Smash dancing as a mural on my bedroom wall; it was brilliant. We grew up in a time when our parents kicked us out at nine o'clock in the morning and told us not to come back until teatime. I loved it. We had an absolute riot and our friendship only got stronger.

It wasn't all bliss, though. I'm not as thick-skinned as I might come across. After a couple of traumatic teenage moments, I started having panic attacks while I was in technical college, which was part of the YTS scheme when I worked for Gordon Stewart. I'd been going out with this girl called Emma, my first real proper love. It lasted about a year before she dumped me. It was unceremonious, I mean really. She dropped me from a very great height, probably because I didn't fit in with her social circle. Maybe that's why being accepted by the antiques trade (which is a tight-knit, often very snobby community) has been so important to me. Even as a kid, acceptance was something I think I yearned for, and it hurt like hell when Emma ditched me.

I tried to get over it by throwing myself into the rebuild of my first car, a Morris Minor two-door, which I bought in 1985 when I was only 15. It took a couple of years and when it was finished it didn't have any seat belts. I'd put massive 'Carlos Fandango' wheels on the back and a bucket seat which wasn't bolted to the floor properly. There was a tiny steering wheel with no horn and the first time I took it for a proper run was across the valley to see Chris Holt with T. It was raining hard and the road pretty slick when we came around the other side of the valley. The car was going really well, then these lads passed us in a MK II Ford Escort and I remember thinking, Fucking hell, I'm having them. I stamped on the accelerator pedal, caught them up and tried to overtake but the car skidded sideways before properly rolling over. Amazingly, we didn't have so much as a scratch. Later, T told me he knew exactly how many times we had rolled because the beanie hat he wore back then kept disappearing and reappearing. Two and a half times in all. We should've been dead, because the roof caved in, the back window was gone and the engine was still running. I could smell petrol and when I looked over my shoulder I saw that the fuel tank was leaking and petrol was filling up the roof. Instinct must've kicked in because I immediately turned the ignition off, got myself out and kicked in T's window. A man and his kids pulled up in their car after they saw what happened and drove us to T's parents' house, telling us it was like watching something from the telly.

Neither of us had been injured physically, but I had a delayed reaction. A couple of days after the crash I was at work in the cement shed when I started to feel sort of tingly and out of body. It was really odd. I couldn't understand what was going on. Suddenly I couldn't cope and I had no idea what was happening. It was very scary and it was only much later that I realised it was trauma, which had started with the breakup from Emma and then the car crash. But I didn't know it then. I was working on a piece of glass when something just welled up inside me. I couldn't breathe. I was trembling. I had this weird feeling of panic. I didn't know what to do; it got worse and worse, I started to hyperventilate, so I went outside to get some air. Gordon took one look and told me to go home. Someone gave me a lift and, when I got to the house, I told my father I was feeling really weird and couldn't understand what was happening.

'You're just mental,' he said.

Right, brilliant. That's really going to help. I don't know why I bothered to tell him.

I managed to calm myself down and, after a couple of days, I seemed to be OK. But as time went on it kept happening. I was at a loss. There was no internet to look things up on and I didn't want to go to the doctor and tell him what I was feeling because I really didn't know myself. How could I say that one minute I was alright and the next I felt like I was going to die? No doctor would understand that, not in the 1980s. So, I didn't see anyone, I just tried to deal with it myself and it took me years to figure out what was happening. I was suffering from anxiety and these were panic attacks. It began with my girlfriend and was exacerbated by rolling the car; two major disturbances that followed one right after the other.

That was 33 years ago and I still suffer from them today. When an attack hits I have to meter it through until I'm over it. I understand what's going on but it's debilitating and can completely stop you in your tracks. I'm not a weak man. I've had to deal with all kinds of setbacks, but when a panic attack hits, it can knock me right on my arse.

It's hard to identify exactly what sets it off; it can be all sorts of things, and some that creep up on you when you least expect it. Being around too many people can do it, being pulled this way and that either in business or emotionally. I think part of the attraction of buying the chapel was the remote location, which meant I'd be able to shut myself away and get on with it. I did that for years, but I still suffered from panic attacks and some-times they'd hit when I was on the chapel roof and that was a bit scary. There was no one around to see what I was going through, though, and I didn't talk about it to anyone because I didn't want anyone to judge me. It took another ten years before I went to the doctor, and by then the world was a different place entirely. Men had finally started to talk about things that affected them, and mental health was no longer taboo. The doctor knew what was going on and was very sympathetic. Initially, she pre-scribed some drugs and taught me breathing exercises and different coping mechanisms.

Quite a few of my friends have suffered similarly and most of them have no clue what's going on. Rather than feeling ashamed now, I can explain what's happening and help them get through it. A close friend started having attacks about a year ago; she called me up and I just told her we'd stay on the phone until it was sorted. Panic attacks are not something I ever expected to suffer from, but they're part of my life, and I've learned to live with them. It's not easy but at least now there's no stigma attached and that makes talking about it much less difficult.

CHAPTER 5

LIFE, LOVE AND LOWS

With my previous girlfriend having left, I spent the years between 25 and 29 with Blue, my beloved collie, working on the church, and I was as happy as I've ever been. Other girl-friends came and went, but the only residents were the two of us. Slowly but surely, I realised the dream I'd envisioned when I first went up there with Andy. I created something out of the chapel house and, when it was complete, I let it out and moved into the derelict two-storey stable block. Gradually that morphed into a very nice holiday cottage that was so popular, by the time I stopped renting it out, it was occupied for 50 weeks of the year.

So, the house was done and that was followed by the chapel. I'd turned 28 by now and had two sets of paying tenants. Back to basics again, I moved into the chapel and slept on an old mattress. Every day after work, I'd be up on the roof working, and every day this same girl would drive by in a white VW Golf and beep the horn at me. I was very fit back then, thin and muscular: she must've liked what she saw.

One night I fancied some company so I went down to the local pub. As I walked in, I saw the girl from the Golf sitting in a corner with her mates. I found out her name was Kate and she was half-Irish. We got talking, one thing led to another and a few months after we started seeing each other I found out she was pregnant. A year older than me, she already had two boys and it came as a massive shock because I never had any thoughts about having children – it wasn't part of the plan.

I had to think logistics, though, and with the chapel house and stable block finished, I told Kate I'd ask the ten-ants to vacate and we'd move in. I liked her sons, both good lads, so it wouldn't be a problem. Decision made, a few weeks later we went for a scan at Bodelwyddan Hospital on the other side of Abergele. By now I was into the idea of fatherhood and looking forward to a way of life I'd not even contemplated. But something changed in Kate and the plans went right out the window.

These days, my son Tom works in the shop during the summer and he plans to go into the auctioneering business when he finishes his degree. We have a brilliant relation-ship but it's one I had to fight for. All those years ago when Kate told me she was pregnant we'd only been together six months and that's too short a time to really get to know someone you might spend the rest of your life with. I was still in shock the day we went for the scan, wondering how I was going to pull it together. It was daunting, but at the same time I was up for it. Now this had happened, all I wanted to do was be a good father. I didn't get the chance, though. Far from moving in together, by the time Tom was born, his mother and I weren't even seeing each other. For various reasons, the relationship broke down before it ever began, but I made sure I was at the birth, conscious that it might not be something I'd experience again. I remember just hoping there would be nothing wrong with him and, thankfully, there wasn't. He was fit and healthy, and we named him Tom James Hamilton-Pritchard, which was a combination of his mother's name and mine. Tom was my grandfather on my mother's side who fought in the Second World War. Back home in Wales afterwards, he was reunited with my grandmother 'Nin' only to drop dead in the kitchen of a brain aneurysm. Nin never married again; for 50 years she remained true to his memory, and that was something I really respected. A formidable, wonderful woman who was always 'Nin' because I couldn't pronounce 'Nainy' (what we call grandmothers in North Wales) when I was a young child. Five foot of fury, she used to 'force-feed' T whenever he came round, because he was so thin and pasty. Nin was a massive influence on my life; it's not exaggerating to say she shaped it.

After Tom was born, communication between me and his mother was non-existent. She'd gone from being the person I was going to share my life with to someone else. I was 29 and still working from the partitioned inspection pit underneath my dad's garage. In that tiny space I was restoring stained glass and stripping doors, as well as selling old fireplaces and windows. I had a lean-to shed at the bottom of the garden to store stuff and a little sign on the road that said 'Stained Glass – Architectural Antiques'. Things between me and Kate had completely broken down; Tom was five months old and I was fighting for the right to see him. I was living in the chapel and driving to my parents' house for work.

Looking back, I let that situation go on far too long, because years before my relationship with my father had broken down completely. It was one of those things that just happened. There was no single event to spark it off – it was just a gradual deterioration that I've never been able to get to the bottom of. Initially he really did encourage me, but the more I got into the business of antiques the more estranged we seemed to become. I didn't understand it then and I still don't now.

I used to work for him cutting log signs all day on a Saturday. We had a huge circular saw with no guard on it; a massive thing, it was fucking dangerous. A 60cm-diameter blade with teeth the size of a pair of adult thumbs, I'd use it to cut planks of yew for house names he'd sign-write for customers. I'd work until I was knackered, cutting and shaping, sanding the wood and varnishing. That saw was lethal, there's no way I'd go anywhere near it now and I was only 11 years old. Every Saturday and all through the summer holidays I'd work until I dropped, yet it felt like all he did was have a go at me.

I haven't seen him in 16 years. I see my mum all the time and she reckons all he talks about is how he wants to see me. I've tried to do that over the years, but we're at each other's throat within about thirty seconds of meeting. I think he believes I don't know anything that he didn't teach me, but the truth is I taught myself. It's a tragedy what's happened between us. I think he's an amazing man; he can play 13 different instruments and is a brilliant fine artist. He's completely self-taught in everything he does. I just wish he could acknowledge the same in me.

By this time my relationship with Kate was well and truly over. The deterioration began with the scan at the hospital, and it seemed to finish before it ever really got started. But I had a son, and within six months of him being born I met Rebecca.

I was in the workshop at my parents' house working with Darren restoring some glass, and the only natural light was the head-height window. I was taking a break when this knackered old Volvo 940 estate turned up, the driver's door opened and this woman got out with razor-cut peroxide hair. She was wearing a big baggy jumper, a pair of skin-tight black leather trousers and a pair of biker-style jackboots. As soon as I saw her I turned to Darren and said, 'I'm going to marry her.'

I went out to see what she wanted and she told me she'd bought a 40-acre farm near Betws-y-Coed and needed some shutters for the windows on the farmhouse. I didn't have anything like that, but I fancied the pants off her, so I showed her a few shitty old doors just to keep the conversation going. I found out later she was a few years older than me, but she didn't look her age, in fact she looked way younger than I did. Determined to see her again, I took a phone number and told her I'd find what she wanted.

A few weeks later I phoned her up and told her I'd located the stuff and would bring it out to the farm. By then I was driving a Jeep Cherokee, which was the first modern car I'd ever owned. When I found out I was going to be a dad, I thought I'd better have a sensible car, so I bought a four-litre, manual, left-hand-drive Jeep that did about three miles to the gallon. After loading the shutters and other bits and bobs I'd picked up, I put my last 20 quid's worth of fuel in the tank and drove out to her place at Betws-y-Coed. I'm not joking; that's the only money I had. I was skint now, completely. I had a mortgage to pay and didn't know how I was going to do it. Every penny I earned I spent on the chapel. If I made 50 quid, I didn't think about feeding myself, I bought roof slates or floor tiles. When I bought the place, I'd had a vision of what it would be, and if I spent 400 quid, I knew I'd be adding £4,000.

When I got to Rebecca's place, bizarrely, her mum and sister were there and we sat down and had a chat; I discovered she was divorced with two young daughters. A few weeks later she came over to the chapel and we spent the weekend together and that was pretty much the two of us from then on.

Six months after that first weekend with Rebecca, I moved to her farm in Betws-y-Coed, which was still a work-in-progress. What I loved about her was the can-do, no-fear attitude she always had: for Bec there was no such thing as an insurmountable obstacle. Spread over 43 acres was the farmhouse, campsite and holiday cottage, plus a B&B as well as two caravans. She'd taken on the project all by herself while trying to bring up two young children. I helped her do the place up and gradually it began to come together. What I'd told Darren that morning turned out to be true. I did marry her and she got involved with the business. Her daughters eventually changed their surname to mine and effectively became my children.

The next few years sucked the life right out of me. Whatever I tried to do for my son Tom, it seemed I was thwarted. I wanted him to go to a decent school, one I could afford to pay for, and it took a huge amount of effort and emotion just to get agreement for that to happen. I never said anything to Tom, whatever issues go on between parents should be kept well away from the children. Suffice to say, I'll do anything I can to support Fathers 4 Justice. That whole period was a real low point in my life and, unfortunately, it was to be repeated in terms of my relationship with Rebecca. The difference this time, though, was that what happened between us was entirely my fault, and I take full responsibility for it. People drift apart, and there are a lot of factors involved, one of which is not spending enough quality time together, and that was certainly the case with us. The travelling I have to continually do meant I was often away from home, which inevitably put pressure on the relationship, but the way it unravelled wasn't necessary. It could have been done in a much more grown-up manner, but I behaved like an idiot. I let the fact that nobody seemed to be saying 'no' to me any more go completely to my head, albeit only for a brief moment. It's not something I'm proud of and I regret my actions bitterly, but with hindsight we *were* growing apart and the decision to split was the right one.

By the time our marriage was over we'd long since moved from the farm at Betws-y-Coed to the converted chapel in the Conwy Valley. The hassle of running a B&B and campsite had taken its toll on both of us and we were fed up of people not treating the place with any respect. For some reason the customers didn't seem to care about their surroundings; they would try to cut down trees for campfires and leave litter all over the place; it was incredibly frustrating. Camp grounds have to be appealing and it was just too much work constantly clearing up after the guests. We'd be up at the crack of dawn and never in bed before midnight and every day just seemed to run into the next.

Once we moved on from Betws-y-Coed, things should have been great and for a while they were: we had a fantastic place to live, with everything I'd envisaged when I first bought the chapel having been completed. It wasn't just the buildings; I'd bought more land so there was a massive garden where I could take a day to mow the lawn if I wanted. I was around for the school run and I had all my old cars to mess about with. But by now the TV show was becoming pretty successful and, as a result, we were filming more and more episodes and that meant I started to be away more than I was at home.

Business was great, and not just because of the show: in those days I had almost a floor of my own at Liberty in London, which was pretty much unheard of. It took up so much time that we leased a flat in Chelsea so Rebecca could manage that part of the business. We would both be home most weekends, but that was the only real time we'd have together and I know I wasn't attentive enough. I didn't take care of our relationship. I loved being with the children, that was always great and I'd be there for them as much as I could, but problems started to arise between me and Rebecca. We both had a hell of a lot to do, with her in London and me filming, and trying to get back into the rhythm of dealing was getting ever more difficult. Initially, the show only took up 10 per cent of my time, but as the series grew more successful the demands increased and today it's more like 90.

That growth was exponential and so was the downward spiral in terms of my behaviour. By the time we got to series eight, I was on the road all the time, staying in a different hotel every night with nothing to do but hit the bar. I've never been one to shut myself away so, as I alluded to before, drinking started to become an issue. It was particularly bad at the weekends when I'd get stuck into the red wine, and that was the beginning of my downfall. The funny thing is I'd never been bothered about alcohol before. I didn't really start drinking at all until I was 29, it didn't interest me. I might have a couple of pints on a Friday night with the lads, but that was it. After we started making the show, though, I began to drink every night and for a while it was a little crazy; we were working hard during the day nailing every show, but come the evening it was a debacle, really. Almost overnight, I started drinking a lot of beer during the week and, come the weekend, I could open a bottle of red wine and ten minutes later it would be empty. I'd happily do another and sometimes start on a third and that was only the tip of the iceberg. Every Friday night, every Saturday and Sunday, I would neck bottles of red wine on my own and it did not go unnoticed.

Rebecca could see how it was beginning to get out of hand and it wasn't very long before she told me I needed to do something about it. I knew she was right, but I didn't want to listen. Her opinion no longer mattered because emotionally I'd already left the marriage. I was there in body but not much else and it was becoming apparent to everyone. My heart was no longer in it. I was unhappy and I don't know why. I loved the house and I loved the children, but things were changing in other parts of my life and I was trying to make the adjustment. I was no longer just an antique dealer. I had a TV show, and trying to balance the time and commitment between the two wasn't easy. The bottom line was I was unhappy in both my marriage and the business. It felt like the show was taking over and I was getting pulled further and further away from the day-to-day dealing. Rebecca and I argued about it. I was spread too thin and that creates a feeling of being out of control, which wasn't helped by the panic attacks. The arguments grew more frequent and heated and it was my fault. I was changing, becoming a different person, and the amount of red wine I was drinking had a profound effect on who that person turned out to be.

I tried to keep tabs on it while we were working but, as I said above, for a while at least, it did get a little out of hand. I remember one day when we finished filming, I got to the hotel before the crew as they had to pack up all the equipment and I wanted to get stock uploaded to the website. By this time, we were staying in decent hotels and this was a really swanky place. I hit the bar an hour before T got there and, when he walked in, I was already into a third or fourth pint. Dinner didn't happen, and by half-seven I was so hammered he had to walk me up the stairs, pour me into my room and point me towards the bed.

I always complied with the 12-hour ban on drinking in the run up to filming, but it carried on like that for a while. I made the call-sheet every day and did what I was being paid to do. When we started to go abroad it was harder. An away day in a different country with new people to meet and new places to see, it was a licence to drink and my life became a swirl of filming and booze then going home to a place I didn't want to be.

Somewhere in the middle of all that I made a massive mistake. I got involved with another woman and that really wasn't good for me. I knew I was messing up badly but that didn't stop me. I was out of control. I was hurting people I didn't want to hurt and it took far too long for the penny to drop. By the time it did, in 2016, my relationship with Rebecca was beyond repair, as it was abundantly clear I didn't want to be there. I knew I couldn't allow it to go on, so I got myself together enough to sit down with her and tell her I wanted a divorce.

'Fine,' she said. 'Me too.'

That conversation should've allowed me the space to think so the two of us could do what had to be done in a grown-up way, but it wasn't like that. Instead of calming me down, it was as if someone had taken the shackles off. I didn't have to pretend any more. I didn't have to be someone

I didn't want to be. I went wild, and I mean absolutely crazy. I began to party like there was no tomorrow. I had money in my pocket and I was on my own again. In a single month I spent £18,000 on hotel bills, hanging out with all sorts of people I really should've avoided. I was hammering it badly, drinking at least three bottles of red wine a night and beginning to make myself ill. It got so bad that eventually I went to the doctor, and he did a liver and kidney test to find out the kind of damage I was doing. When the results came in, he sat me down and told me that I would die if I didn't stop drinking immediately. I don't know whether I believed him or not. I probably thought he was exaggerating.

'Fine,' I said. 'Right, I'll pack it in then. I can do that, no problem.' But I didn't. I wasn't an alcoholic. I didn't need AA meetings or rehab. I *wanted* to drink; I didn't have to. I didn't stop. I pushed what had been said to the back of my mind and carried on just as before. That went on for a few more months, then, suddenly, something clicked and I knew I had to stop. I didn't pack it in altogether, but I immediately quit the red wine. That was my poison, it's what changed my behaviour, so I knocked it on the head and stopped partying every night.

With the consumption of red wine in check, I could see what this crazy lifestyle had done to me. I'd lost my house, my wife and my children. I was so out of it most of the time my buying instincts were all over the place and I nearly lost my business as well. The whole period is still a haze.

There are weeks that I can't recall and I don't know if that was caused by the drink or if I just don't want to remember what happened. It's as if it was happening to someone else where the timeline makes no sense, and I can't remember half the things people tell me I got up to. Drinking too much also brought on panic attacks – it was a real mess.

I hate myself for allowing the situation to get out of hand, and I bitterly regret the hurt I caused to Rebecca. To this day I don't have any idea why I behaved as I did. I have no real idea what made me start drinking so much. I have no idea why I went off with another woman or why I spent so much money on stuff that wasn't good for me. I can't explain why I caused so much pain to the people that were closest to me. I look in the mirror and have no answer to the questions I ask myself. It was just something that happened.

But self-destruction had run its course and I was able to save the business. Trade was crap – so bad, in fact, I was using my savings to pay the ten grand I had to shell out every month in wages. I was trying to make sense of the fact we weren't taking any money and it hit me when I walked into the warehouse one day and saw the quality of the stock. I had no idea how so much rubbish had got there and nobody could understand what was going on. When I took a moment to think it through, the answer was obvious. I'd been buying online while shit-faced on red wine and the result was an inventory we'd never get rid of.

CHAPTER 5

It brought me up short and I started to sort things out both professionally and personally. I got back to buying the right stock and the business began to pick up again. At the same time, Rebecca and I went through the divorce proceedings. I knew I was at fault so I didn't want to fight her on anything. I basically told her she could have whatever she wanted and that included the chapel, which was already on the market with an asking price of £895,000. I remember standing up in court and telling her she could have it all. I wasn't going to contest anything. We had no mortgage and I was entitled to half the value of the marital home but I felt total guilt so I just gave it to her. The only thing she didn't take were my cars. She could have, they were part of our possessions, but she didn't seem to want them. Worth a lot of money at that time, there were 13 sports and vintage cars, and I still don't know why she left them. I bought her out of the business (which was a considerable sum in cash) and gave her an alimony settlement. It took months to sort out, a very difficult period for both of us, and during it all we were still filming the TV series.

Single again, I was on my uppers completely. Having had a stack of money in the bank, I had barely anything to my name now. I was out of the chapel and had to sell a car so I had enough cash to put a small deposit on a house in Conwy. That was it, though, an empty house where I had nothing but a single Howard sofa in front of the fire and

Enzo my faithful Jack Russell. For weeks he and I ate out of the same can and he curled up with me on that sofa.

I was still pretty unaware just how bad my behaviour had become; it was only much later that I realised how big an idiot I'd actually been. Maybe deep down somewhere there's a big red self-destruct button that's begging to be pressed and every so often I have to oblige it. I try to tell myself that it had no effect on the TV, but that's not true. Although I never missed a call, I know if I'd been in a better space, we would have made a better show.

To write it down like this is cathartic, but it's also pretty disturbing. Somehow, I got through it, and the irony is that during that 'blizzard' period, we had some of the best viewing figures we've ever achieved. It was rock 'n' roll and nobody was saying 'no' to me. I'd walk into a hotel and be recognised by the staff and there was nothing they couldn't do to make my stay more comfortable. A free upgrade on the room, Mr Pritchard? Sure. A bottle of champagne, Mr Pritchard? Why not? Anything I wanted they gave me. It was intoxicating and I immersed myself in the lifestyle completely.

The fact there was no rhyme or reason to any of it still bothers me. The way it just crept up with no warning is a worry, because if it happened once it can happen again. If I was able to see a sequence of events that led up to the blow-out, I know I'd be able to avoid it. But I can't. There is no point in time where I can say: That happened, and, as a result I did this, or X led to Y and so on.

CHAPTER 5

Anyway, it was all over thankfully, and I had to begin again. This time was different, though; there was no Rebecca to help me, I'd have to do it on my own. Now I'm out the other side I regret what happened and the way it happened, but I don't regret the decision to leave the marriage because it had run its course for both of us. Instead of getting hammered every night to mask my unhappiness, though, I should've acknowledged it for what it was and sat down with Rebecca much sooner.

CHAPTER 6

BEWARE OF
THE DOG

With no let-up in the TV shooting schedule, T and I spent a few days in Cambridgeshire in early August 2019 on a variety of calls, one of which was the Duxford Aviation Society Museum, which is right up there with the V&A in terms of a fantastic experience. As soon as I found out Concorde was there, I knew I had to have something from the period. That aircraft is iconic, spectacular in both engineering and design. It first flew in 1969 and, to this day, there hasn't been a better-looking commercial plane. At Duxford I was fortunate enough to take the pilot's seat, and to be able to sit in a place of such authority completely blew my mind.

Our guide for the day was a wonderful man called David who is chair of the DAS. I asked him if there were any items of memorabilia left from the plane, an ashtray or something, maybe. He told me all the stuff like that was long gone, but he did think he'd be able to come up with something. In the holding area he went through a set of drawers and found an unused pair of mechanic's overalls with 'CONCORDE' printed on the back. They were amazing: I knew I could sell them all day long and parted with 200 quid. We picked up four BOAC shoulder bags for twenty-five quid apiece; retro-looking, they'd either been for the cabin crew or first-class freebies. There was a lot of other stuff to look through and I found an original blueprint for a Lancaster bomber that took my breath away. 'Look at this, T,' I said. 'Once it's framed, I know collectors who'll be all over it.'

Something else caught my eye, a navigator's seat that I was sure came out of a bomber. 'What's this, David?' I said.

'I'm not sure.' He inspected the seat very carefully. 'The label says Haynes, and that might be from a test. I don't think it's actually from an operational bomber. By the look of it, it's more likely to be an engineer's seat from a test aircraft.'

Even so, there was something about it. 'How much d'you want for it?' I said.

'Three hundred.'

'I tell you what; it's not exactly what I thought it was – how about two-fifty?'

'That's fine,' he said, and we shook on it.

Prior to Duxford, we'd filmed from the spire of Ely Cathedral, T and I schlepping up so many steps my knees were screwed and I thought I was going to die of a heart attack. Ely is magnificent, a work of art in terms of architecture and built on the site of a church that dates back to AD 672. Again, our guide was called David and he told us the stone had been quarried at Barnack and bought from Peterborough Abbey. I could see elements of Purbeck marble from the fossil beds down in Dorset, as well as an ancient building material they call clunch, which is a chalky limestone only found in Normandy and the east of England. I was here to buy as well as study the architecture, though, and spotted something that stopped my breath. Two seven-foot wooden pews; one was very badly damaged but the other was complete and it was a belter.

'Is that Gilbert Scott?' I asked David.

'It is,' he said. 'We're very proud to have it.'

No wonder. This was a find-and-a-half, a pew from the Aesthetic/Gothic-style restoration and remodel of Ely by George Gilbert Scott, a prolific 'Revival' architect of the day. I knew his work, but what was more important to me was that the pew had been completed in the style of A.W.N. Pugin. To me, Pugin is pretty much God and I'd come across him when I began to appreciate the stained glass wrought by William Morris. I had to have this; it was just one of those pieces you never find and it wouldn't go to the shop or website. I wanted it for the house I knew I would buy as soon as I found it. Ever since I left the chapel, I've had the house I want in my head only – I've yet to actually locate it. Despite that, I'm already filling the rooms with various items I'll never sell, and the Gilbert

Scott pew was one of them. I asked David how much he wanted for it.

'We couldn't let it go for less than a thousand.'

'I'll give you a thousand,' I said. 'How about two hundred for the one that's broken?'

'Alright,' he said. 'We can do that.'

I'd been to Ely once before as a kid. Back then, however, I knew nothing of the history and that's what the antiques business is all about. You learn in steps; a little bit of this, a little bit of that, and as the years go by you amass a great deal of knowledge. I've said it before, but that's what grabbed me when I began to read the catalogues and Lyle books Mum and Dad had around the house. I mentioned them before, but I'm not quite sure I got across just how important they were to me and how much time I actually spent studying. Unlike schoolwork, where I couldn't see the point, I devoured every Lyle and catalogue I could get my hands on. They excited me then and they still excite me today because you can never learn enough, there's always something else going on. Knowledge is critical, not just so you have a handle on what an item is worth, but for the appreciation of the artistry and history. There's a soul to this business and I can't reiterate enough just how much that means to me. I take what I do very seriously. I still pinch myself when I think how far I've come in terms of understanding and appreciation.

I thought back to what T had said about flying a drone over Piccadilly Woods. There's no reason why the remnants of those old cars shouldn't be back there. It would've been hard to clear them from the farmland above and the builders of the housing estate completely ignored them. The idea that some bits and pieces might still be there really excites me because I relate the time when I saw cars floating in the air with the Gilbert Scott restoration at Ely Cathedral. Links in a chain; you understand *this* then you learn about *that* and, over time, those snippets of information start meshing together. One day you might be looking at nineteenth-century English furniture, and the day after that Georgian chimneypieces. You see a pattern form in terms of when things were made and what was in the mind of the people that made them.

Not all dealers have that level of appreciation; some are just there to turn a profit. One who does, though, is Peter Whipps, who we filmed with after a night at the Belfry, where we'd stopped on the way from Cambridgeshire. Though I hate golf with a passion, the Belfry makes a good burger, so I ate one of those then spent the evening loading more stuff onto the website, including the chest of drawers I'd bought from Sir James Shuckburgh. Kevin had completed the work and it looked fantastic. I stayed up late making sure everything had been taken care of, so I wasn't too bothered when I got a call telling me filming had been delayed in the morning.

Peter rents space from the Dugdale Estate in Warwickshire, a couple of barns next door to a lovely old Tudor farmhouse that's rented by a lady called June who keeps St Bernard dogs. The crew were due to get there before T and I showed up in the van and first on scene was Simon Jolly. He's the sound man and has been with us since the very first TV show; he's the third Salvage Hunter along with T and me. He's brilliant at his job and his being first on set wasn't unusual, but he had no idea the farmhouse didn't belong to Peter.

'What's up?' I said when the director phoned me. 'Why the delay?'

'It's Simon. Anna just took him to A&E.'

I was still in bed, adding yet more items we'd bought and restored to the website.

'He's been bitten by a dog. Peter Whipps found him; the dog almost took his hand off.'

'Is he OK?'

'I don't know. They've taken him to have an X-ray.'

'How did a dog manage to bite him?'

'He thought the farmhouse was Peter's. The dogs were loose and he stuck his hand over the fence to stroke them.'

Fucking idiot, the first thing I saw when we pulled up in the van later was a sign on the farmhouse gate. BEWARE OF THE DOG. ENTER AT YOUR OWN RISK. I could see two bloody great St Bernards locked up in a cage and they were barking at me. When Simon got there, they'd been loose and he'd been daft enough to reach over the gate. Not only that, he'd locked his keys in his van and we were waiting for the AA. When Anna, the assistant producer, brought him back from hospital with his hand all bandaged up, he looked pale and shocked and showed me a photo of the wound on his phone. A massive great gash across the top of his wrist, it looked as if the hand was about to fall off. Of course, I gave him all the sympathy I could muster.

'You didn't see the sign then?' I said to him.

'No.'

'It's right there on the farmhouse gate.'

'Yeah, but the dogs were friendly.'

'Evidently.' I nodded to the mass of bandage.

'No, I mean they were wagging their tails and everything. This is a dog-friendly show. I thought the dogs were Peter's; I didn't think anything of it.'

'How many were there?'

'Four.'

'Well, if it was going to happen to someone, it was going to happen to you. Four massive dogs and you put your hand in?'

He was looking sheepish. 'Well, no. I said hello first.'

'Oh yeah, cos dogs can understand that, can't they?'

I did feel for him, of course I did; but it was a stupid thing to do and the crew were taking the piss. Steve, the lead cameraman, located an advert for Jollyes Dog Food on the net which he immediately forwarded to Simon.

With Simon out of action for the day, we had to wait for another sound man but also the AA. In the meantime, T and

I took a look around the studio where Peter photographs his stock. He's only been selling online for about six years, prior to that he relied on people coming out here or visiting the shop in Tetbury. He's been in the business twenty-odd years, starting out in what we call 'Country' furniture, exemplified by the kind of untouched cupboards and cabinetry you see in old English country houses. After that he moved more into 'Original Paint', which are items that have been decorated. One of his mainstays is garden antiques and, as we walked in, a large terracotta urn caught my eye. I had a customer in mind with a particular set-up he wanted to exploit and I thought this might fit the bill exactly.

'So, it was you who found Simon then?' I said to Peter.

He nodded. 'The crew told me they'd be here between eight and half-past but he arrived before then. When I pulled up, there was blood everywhere.'

Peter's wife Dawn was making tea while the crew set up and Simon sat down to nurse his wounds and wait for the AA. Dawn is as much involved in the trade as her husband, having started a company called Arabesque Interiors years ago. Since then she's been a mural artist and worked on restoration with Peter, as well as designing interiors. Now she buys and sells twentieth-century paintings.

Peter had to make a couple of calls so T and I took a look at the stuff in his showroom, a really nice barn with a beamed pitch roof over a set of double glass doors that creates a feeling of light and space. He had some cracking stuff, including a George III washstand that had been dry-scraped to clear what was probably a dozen layers of paint. If you're lucky you can scrape a piece like that back to its original layer, but it takes a lot of man-hours. You might find unpainted pine in rustic pieces but not generally from those country houses. There the furniture was always painted: sometimes to enable a piece to fit with the room but sometimes it was just decorative. In the late eighteenth and early nineteenth century, country houses were flamboyant and whenever you find something like this you take a punt on whether you can take it back to the condition it should be. It's immensely time-consuming and costly but whoever worked on the washstand had done a great job.

Peter had another piece that looked freshly scraped, a George III cupboard that was missing its handles. I put it around 1780: good looking, well built with good proportions. Like most English cupboards of the period, it stood really well, with the kind of simplicity you don't find in European examples. I found a really handsome Regency Waterfall bookcase and Peter told me he'd already spent 600 quid on the dry-scrape and it barely looked like it had been touched.

'Where'd you get it?' I asked him.

He smiled a little wryly. 'I bought it in a sale. Someone had added a couple of drawers and it was catalogued as a kitchen dresser. I only paid four hundred quid for it.'

CHAPTER 6

It just goes to show that the salerooms don't always know what they've got. This was one of the best examples of a Regency Waterfall I'd seen. The form was excellent, and even with the cost of dry-scraping Peter would see an excellent profit.

He really does have a good eye. Standing against one wall was a great Welsh dresser in dark oak, the sort of piece I always look to buy. This one would probably be too expensive, but I did want a cabinet for an interior designer who was working on a house in Beverly Hills. That's the beauty of the website, since that Eureka moment with Rob Wilding 20 years ago, I've created a database that spans the globe. Peter's not been exploiting it for as long as I have, but he's one of the best architectural antique dealers in the country. He understands what he's looking at and loves things in the same condition as I do, which is pretty much untouched. Dry-scraping is a chore alright, but the result is worth it. Sometimes it's done with a very sharp chisel, sometimes something as simple as a two-pence piece. Peter's a purist; the way the stuff was displayed was clever and educated, it had a really good look that was reflected in the quality of each item.

He had a couple of urns set up on socles (which is the base they sit on). There was a pair of early-nineteenth-century stocks and a selection of glass cucumber straighteners. These were copies of originals that George Stephenson (of Stephenson's *Rocket*) had blown in his Northumberland factory. Like most Victorian inventors, Stephenson tried to adapt the natural world to his own design and had a thing about the curve in a cucumber. He wanted his to be straight so he had a competition with his neighbour to see who could grow the best one. He had the glass blown specifically with a hole in the top where a string was tied and the young cucumber attached to it. The glass was then hung in a greenhouse and as the cucumber grew it was shaped by the confines of the cylinder. Peter told us he'd found them in a derelict greenhouse in somebody's garden and now they were displayed in a hand-barrow made by William Woods of Taplow.

'How much do you want for them?' I asked him.

'The whole lot are up at fourteen hundred. I had a couple a few years ago but sold them and didn't think I'd see any more until I got the call about the greenhouse.'

That was too steep for me, so I took a closer look at the urns, which were Coade stone, the pinnacle of English terracotta. The name comes from Eleanor Coade, who was in the business of making garden statuary in the late eighteenth century. She created a process called Lithodipyra, the twice-firing of terracotta that was ground down so it could be poured into moulds to create neoclassical urns and statues. The designs were created by the cream of English sculptors, people like John Bacon, famous for his bust of George III in Oxford and Father Thames at Ham House near Richmond. If you walk across Westminster Bridge, you can see eight Bacon Coade stone urns on top of Somerset House. Eleanor Coade was a visionary; a businesswoman in the days when they were few and far between. She came from a family that were both wool merchants and weavers, though, so it was in her DNA. I checked out the Pulham urns that were Victorian from Suffolk, where James Pulham's company specialised in rock gardens and follies. They used terracotta and something they created called Pulhamite which had been inspired by Coade stone from the previous century.

We continued to look around and T spotted some Coalbrookdale cast-iron urns that were 'Naples' in design, meant to create an Italian feel. One other piece really stood out, a classic example of chinoiserie, a chest on a stand in black and gold; it was absolutely beautiful.

'Where's that from?' I asked Peter.

'Uttar Pradesh.'

'1850?'

'About then, yes. It's got the original key, the original folding stands so you can move it around. Lovely, isn't it?'

'It's a belter.' I opened the chest and it still had the original paint inside. This was the kind of thing you'd find in a stately home or country house; they're usually displayed in the hallway. Chinoiserie is a European style of decoration that mimics ancient Chinese and East Asian art. This one was textured; you could feel the way the decoration was raised and that made the chest even more interesting. He'd want two grand all day long and it was worth every penny, but there'd be no room to manoeuvre for me.

Outside, the AA man had arrived to try to get Simon's van open. A young buff guy, he looked like a red-haired Arnold Schwarzenegger. First, he tried to pick the lock, but that didn't work so he went around to the passenger side where Simon's keys were lying on the seat. The fob lay face up so he fetched some rubber wedges from his van and hammered them into the top of the door frame, then enlarged the space with a pump-up rubber balloon. There was just enough room to get a pair of metal rods inside and he spent the next five minutes trying to get at the fob. Finally, he managed to use the rods to press the button that popped the locks and the doors were open.

Job done, I joined Peter in the other barn where he kept the stuff he was waiting to restore, and this was decorative salvage at its finest. Windows, a pair of door surrounds he was going to turn into mirrors that would fetch between £8,000 and £10,000. I was considering two bronze wall lanterns from the eighteenth century and he was asking £900. They had a Greek key detail and a really crisp upside-down anthemion; that's decorative artwork from ancient Egypt that was adopted by the Greeks and highlighted again in eighteenth-century Europe. They were missing the glass and I was considering a reglaze in proper German mouth-blown, but that was really pricey. It's the sort of thing we used to do when we restored stuff for other dealers. I knew where to get the glass, what colour and style, but it was expensive and I doubted there would be much room left at the end. I decided to leave them for Peter to punt on to another dealer and turned my attention to a slim two-piece dresser/cabinet with a painted decorative finish.

'I do like this sort of thing,' I said. 'I know it's a bit whimsical but I fall for it every now and again.'

'It's pretty, isn't it?' Peter said. 'I only bought it two days ago. I really like the detail on the legs.'

I was thinking about the interior designer and the house in Beverly Hills. The cabinet was painted pine from the early twentieth century and I thought we might do quite well. I'd need Kevin to replace a run of cock-beading as well as a piece of architrave that would have to be manufactured and painted, but it was the only thing required by way of restoration. The cabinet looked like it might've been commissioned by an interior design company called Colefax & Fowler, who are still in business today. The paint was very good and, although it was English and early twentieth century, it looked like the style the French were creating back in the eighteenth.

'How much do I have to pay?'

'Eight-fifty,' Peter said.

I shook my head. 'Can't do that, not with the work. I'll give you seven hundred for it.'

He agreed to that and, with luck, I'd get £1,200 from the designer for the house in the USA. There wasn't that kind of room in the terracotta urn, though, I'd be lucky to see 100 quid profit. That said, there was nothing to be done to it either. It was English from around 1870 and would fit in the house I was thinking of perfectly. The house has various sets of double doors that open all the way through the ground floor and the urn would fit either outside on the approach or in the hallway. It came with a socle that looked 'associated' even though it wasn't the original. Associated is a term we use which means it looks as if the two pieces are meant to fit together or it's similar in age or maker.

'You're asking six-fifty?' I said.

'Yeah.'

'How about six?'

'Alright, I can do that.'

That was good, I knew I could move it on very quickly and there was no work to be done, maybe I'd see 150.

I've mentioned before that the very best antiques are those that strike an immediate emotional chord and there was one in particular I came across that just shouted 'history' at me. In about 2015, we were called to film a piece for the show at a castle on the Welsh/Cheshire border. T wasn't there; I was with Rob Black, who'd become a pretty good mate after our night out in west London. As it happened, it wasn't so much a castle as a turret, the last remaining section of what had been a massive, sprawling construction.

'Would you look at the place?' I said as we pulled up. 'Imagine living here, Rob, it's incredible.' It was beautiful, atmospheric, and I had a really good feeling about the day ahead. That feeling died the moment we walked through the door, however, because inside the place was awful. The owner was a man of vast means and absolutely no taste. He'd redone every single inch of the interior at great expense but the result was just appalling. God knows how much he'd spent; he had handmade rugs, curtains, wallpaper for every room and every bit of it was horrible. It was nothing like I'd expected; the guy had systematically ruined what had been a stunning house – it was a tour de force in bad taste.

I didn't tell him, of course, it was only my opinion and I might have been wrong, but I don't think so. He took us from room to room and it looked like it had been done by a Barbie doll with a tartan fetish. But he was a nice guy, so what could I do? We were filming and, no matter how bad a place might be, you can't tell someone they've got no taste. The owner was very proud and he was chatting away, but there was nothing there I'd put in my house. I was beginning to think this could turn out to be the shittiest call we'd ever made but we soldiered on in the hope of finding something. There was nothing inside I wanted, so I asked if we could look at the outbuildings.

He led us into the garden and, as we walked up the path, I clocked two marble pots just lying in the rosebed.

Ovaloid in form, I knew what they were despite the fact they were half-covered in brambles and had been used to toss cigarette butts in. Goose pimples broke out on my arms. The hairs went mad on the back of my neck. Fuck me, I thought. Two stone wine coolers, not a pair, but associated. One was full of sand, the other bits of rubbish and brimming with rainwater that soaked the fag butts into a mush of tobacco and paper. They were single-piece marble, like ovaloid sinks, one with a gadrooned body.

I didn't say anything because I still didn't quite believe what I was seeing. We were only just into the call and I decided I'd 'notice' them on the way back to the house, but Rob thought I'd missed them completely.

'Oi,' he said. 'Are you fucking blind, Pritchard? Good job you've got me here. You walked right past two wine coolers. What's wrong with you?'

I tried to shut him up with a look, but the owner of the house turned back to where Rob was pointing. I couldn't ignore the coolers now, so I asked the guy what he wanted for them.

'Huh!' he said. 'Those old things, I was going to chuck them in a skip. Give me two hundred quid and you can have them.' He had no idea what they were and he clearly didn't give a shit either. Dealer mentality kicked in and we shook hands on £100 apiece. Usually, if someone is seriously undervaluing something, I say so right away. I'm not in this business to rip people off, but this guy had all the money in the world and really didn't care about the wine coolers.

I had a gut feeling and already I knew there was no way I'd be selling them. I was pretty certain one was from the eighteenth century, but the one with the gadroon might be from a much earlier period.

'Tell me something,' I said to the owner of the house as he led the way to the outbuildings. 'This place is pretty old; I don't suppose there's any Roman involvement?'

'Oh, yeah,' he said. 'There used to be a building next door but it was demolished; some of the earthworks were Roman.'

'Did you find any bits and pieces?'

'Those two sinks you just bought. I've never had any use for them.'

Are you kidding me? Two hundred quid for the pair, I'd have paid two grand if he'd asked me. But he didn't. He knew where they came from so he must've had an idea they could be Roman. As we walked towards the outbuildings, Rob fell in alongside me. 'Fucking hell, Drew. Can you believe it?'

'I know,' I said. 'I clocked them as soon as we walked out the house. I didn't need you to tell me.'

'You're looking at thousands for them.'

'Maybe. I don't know. They're not for sale, Rob. Too interesting. I'm keeping them.'

I still have to pinch myself whenever I look at those wine coolers in my living room. The history, the years that have passed since anybody used them, just blows me away. You do not find Roman cellarettes lying around in people's gardens, but, somehow, I did. I've never actually had the age confirmed but I've shown them to some very knowledgeable dealer friends and they're all convinced the gadroon is Roman. I've had plenty of offers and I sell about 70 per cent of the stuff I buy to the trade, but there's no way I'm parting with the wine coolers.

CHAPTER 7

NOT FOR THE FAINT-HEARTED

As I said in the introduction, this is a business that's as exciting and diverse as the items we come across, but you have to fully embrace it and roll with those punches. It's varied enough that there are plenty of dealers who only deal with the trade. They don't sell to the public at all, and you see the same stuff passing from hand to hand in one long, continuous rotation. There's a joke among us that, if three antique dealers and a chair washed up on a desert island, all three would make a living.

I've mentioned how it used to be a closed shop but it's not like that any more. There are about forty or so dealers who think they're top of the tree and mixing with them is all about having the confidence to do so. That comes from the knowledge I've amassed over the years where I've had to learn to inhabit a lot of different worlds and deal with a lot of very wealthy people. Many are entitled, posh (for want of a better word), and being able to hold my own (which

I can) with them comes down to the first five seconds of meeting. I've had to learn to walk into very wealthy people's houses to talk about buying or restoring things that have been in their family for generations. That's something that took a little mastering because I left school with nothing and 'entitled' wealth can be intimidating to some people, but not me. That said, I've dealt with self-made men who can't even write their own name and have learned to make no distinction. I remember a day when I made one deal with a toothless scrap dealer, another with a billionaire Irish businessman and, finally, some drugged-up rock star who wanted to buy stained glass off me. I sell unusual things, which means unusual clients, and I've had to learn to live in that space along with them.

In the early days I made a point of watching people's nuances and got to be very good at understanding how to be around them. In this business you have to adapt to a given situation and learn how to handle egos. I don't care who anyone is or where they come from. If they have something I want to buy, I'll try to get it at the price that suits me. It's the same when they come to me. I know what I've got and how much it's worth and if you don't want to pay my price don't waste my time. I'm not being arsey. I just can't be bothered with bullshit. I do the TV shows because I want people to get involved and I'm happy to do as much as I can to assist the expansion of the antiques business.

It's not for the faint-hearted, though. You have to be prepared for the ups and downs; it's not some simple transition from hobby to business. The fact you're only making money if someone *wants* something and not if they have to have it can take its toll. Those who really do well are the people who fully comprehend that their particular take on the trade is bound to go in and out of fashion. It's a question of riding out the storms and surviving. My friend George at Brownrigg in Tetbury has a great eye and a great way of doing things. There's Spencer Swaffer in Arundel and Alex MacArthur in Rye. As far as I'm concerned, they're at the top of their own particular game and have been for a long time. I'm good friends with Russ and Mick of 17/21 up in York, as well as David Bedale and Will Fisher, all of whom are as good as anyone out there.

I've been near the very top of this trade, then dropped off only to climb back again, before dropping off a second time. It's like being on a seesaw: sometimes you're so high you're bouncing on the seat and others so low your arse is between your heels on the tarmac. I don't sell things people need, I sell what they want, and when money's tight that's the first thing to go out the window. By the time I was 38, back in 2008, I was worth about three and a half million quid with three good properties, a million quid's worth of antiques, a fleet of cars and three kids in private education. I'd converted the chapel into the most beautiful home and, businesswise, we were absolutely smashing it. I had a

Above and below: Me aged two at my grandmother Nin's house near West Shore Beach, Llandudno

Me aged five outside my dad's garage in Glan Conwy

On one of our art gallery
holidays in Zermatt,
around 1980

Trying out my first BMX
in Glan Conwy, 1983

Cycling in France,
around 1982

With Mum in
Llandudno, 1970

Me and my
younger brother
Guy in Glan Conwy

Me and Nin at my
cousin Alison's wedding

The family at
Alison's wedding

Hanging around Dad's
shed in Conwy, 1975

On holiday in
France, 1986

At Butlin's
Pwllheli, 1979

At Oulton Park, where I saw my first Porsche

Dad's Jaguar XKs – he should never have sold the 150

Driving the MG TD in the Asda car park, 1985

Me with the Beacon Buggy in 1987

Dad's artwork

Collecting driftwood, 1987

Fitting a church window with my mate Gavin in Kinmel Bay, 1990

holiday place in Abersoch, along with a speedboat, even though I hate the sea. The first time I went out, we ran out of petrol and had to get towed in by another boat being sailed by people who actually knew what they were doing. I'm fine when it comes to engines on land, but I had no experience, and I really hate the water. Looking back, I have no idea why I bought the boat in the first place.

I'd also converted a Gothic church into a warehouse and showroom in Llandudno, and I had a massive warehouse in Glan Conwy, both of which were doing cracking business. Things were so good I took off for a couple of weeks, which is something I never do.

Buying that warehouse in Glan Conwy was a milestone, a purchase that changed the perception of my business but put a huge pressure on my resources. A disused garden centre, I bought it after driving past on a daily basis not long after Rebecca and I got married. It looked like it was rapidly going to rack and ruin, so one morning when I had a bit of time, I called in to see if it might be for sale. I was making money and had been looking for premises, so I thought I'd find out how the land lay. The doors were open and I could see a guy sweeping the floor, so I went over and introduced myself.

'This might be a bit cheeky,' I said, 'but I drive past here every day and I wondered if the place was for sale?'

He seemed to think about that as he looked me up and down. 'Are you in the market?'

'I don't know. I might be. How big is it?'

'The site's four acres and there are two sheds totalling forty thousand square feet.'

'That's pretty big.'

'Yes, it is.'

'I've been looking for warehouse facilities and there must be retail permission?'

'There is,' he said. 'We open seven days a week.'

'Are you thinking of selling?'

'I might be, depends what you'd be willing to pay.'

'How much do you want?'

He took a moment to think about that. 'Three hundred and forty thousand, it's yours.'

Not a bad place to start. 'How about two-forty?'

'Three hundred.'

'Two-sixty.'

'The best I can do is two-eighty.'

'Alright, I'll take it,' I told him.

That deal took no more than five minutes and I remember walking out thinking, I own a four-acre site having walked in with a simple question. It wasn't on a whim though; I just followed my instincts and seized an opportunity. I knew I could use one shed as a showroom and the other for restoration and storage. With something that size my business would be taken even more seriously. I was buzzing as I went back to the car, and when I got to the office Rebecca asked me where I'd been.

'I just bought the garden centre in Glan Conwy.'

'You're kidding?'

'No, I'm serious. We've got a four-acre site and two warehouses.'

With that purchase my portfolio came to four properties but, as far as available cash was concerned, I'd used up all my reserves. I was on my arse and that would come back to haunt me.

On that holiday in Abersoch in 2008 I was able to switch off the phone and chill out properly. We were doing between £2,500 and £5,000 per day, seven days a week, in each of the three warehouses and I'd been buying stock like there was no tomorrow. The most I spent in a week was £83,000, which was an absolute fortune. I had no fear. It wasn't a risk. We were making big money and big money needed big inventory. All was well, so I stretched that two weeks into two and a half, and when I got back I asked the lads how they'd been doing. Chris Holt was manager in Glan Conwy and Clive Holland in Llandudno. I went to see Clive first and asked how business had been and how much money he'd taken.

'Two hundred and fifty quid,' he told me.

'What, this morning?'

'No, in total.'

I stood there not quite taking it in. 'You mean that's all you've done since I've been away?'

'Yeah,' he said. 'I'm sorry, Drew. There's all that crap on the news about the banking crisis. Nobody's buying anything.'

Back in the car I drove to Glan Conwy and had the same conversation with Holty. 'How's it been?' I asked him.

He looked grim. 'It's been crap. We've done nothing. Not a sausage.'

It was like being smacked in the face. A big fat zero. 'You're telling me you haven't sold anything in two and a half weeks?'

'That's right,' he said. 'I don't think we've had anyone in the warehouse.'

The recession hit me hard and the banking sector was in crisis. They stopped lending money, some went bust, and governments propped up the rest. It wasn't just the lack of sales that worried me: in order to get the kind of architectural stock I was known for, houses had to be pulled down or renovated and that was about to stop happening. I knew my supply chain was going to be cut off at the knees and there was fuck-all I could do about it. It felt as if somebody just flicked a switch, the world went black and I had 12 employees working full time who had families and mortgages. The gravy train had stopped. I'd worked unbelievably hard to get where I was, so this was going to hurt, and badly. For years I'd be there at seven in the morning and I was still hitting the coalface come midnight. I'd been savvy, made some smart decisions, but in a few short weeks everything was taken away from me. Miles away in America the banks had lent to people on mortgage bonds that were going to cripple them. The wave of panic that created rolled across the Atlantic and smashed right into me.

I looked at the books, got a handle on exactly where we were, and knew I had to make a decision quickly. The day after the lads told me how little they'd done I woke up to Robert Peston, the business editor at the BBC, telling everybody this was the end of everything.

'Will you shut the fuck up,' I shouted at the television. 'You're making things worse. Just stop talking.'

I went into the warehouse, sat down at my desk and made the toughest decision of my life. That day I let all but two of the contracted employees go, but I made sure I looked after everyone and found them new jobs to go to. Only Gavin and Holty stayed and that was only for a while. I'd been back from holiday just one day but the writing was on the wall already. I knew, if I didn't act, I could lose everything. I paid what was owed in wages until the end of the month but that was all I could do. As soon as it was done, I got on the phone to anybody I owed money to and promised to settle their bills, but it would take longer than I'd expected. It was the same promise Gordon Stewart had made to me that Christmas Eve all those years ago. He made good on his word and I would too. I hate it when people go bankrupt and fuck everybody over. I've had it done to me on a couple of occasions and it sucks. I wasn't going to do that. I promised them I'd pay what was owed in full and made sure I did.

The bank didn't help; in fact, they were absolutely useless. Two weeks after the crash I had this snivelling piece of shit sit down in my office with the kind of look on his face that only bankers with final-salary pension schemes can display.

'OK, Mr Pritchard,' he said. 'Things aren't going to get better; we need to do something about it.'

'Hang on,' I said. 'I'm still servicing my loans; in fact, I'm overpaying on both of them.' I've always done that: if I borrow money and the repayment is £1,500 a month, I'll pay £2,500.

'You're paying now,' he said, 'but there's no money coming in. We need the deeds to your house.'

That put the fear of God into me, but it also made me angry. I'd never let anyone put a business charge on my house and I wasn't going to start with this guy.

'No way,' I said. 'That's never going to happen.'

'Alright, but we want our exposure reduced, so the only other option is to sell your commercial properties.'

I should've told him to go fuck himself right there, but I didn't. Instead, I did as he told me. I put some of the properties on the market and sold the storage place right away. The church in Llandudno was wanted by a guy I knew who'd made millions from some dot-com company. He showed up, took a look around and told me he'd pay the full price in cash, but I had to be ready in six weeks.

'Can you do that?'

'Course I can,' I told him.

It was much easier said than done, because the place was crammed full of stock and it cost me thousands to get it shifted. I might as well not have bothered because, just as we were about to complete, he started playing silly buggers and I had to pay the mortgage for another year. He'd gone back on his word but couldn't give a shit. Finally, we did complete but, in the meantime, I was losing a fortune paying the bills on both premises while we took in no money. They talk about a double-dip recession, but I was bitten once, then again before it came back for a third go. With one property sold and one supposedly sold, I had the garden centre, one Transit van and my old Mercedes estate, which was completely shot to shit. My Porsche went, all the other cars went, along with the holiday home and speedboat I'd never wanted in the first place. I still had help from Rebecca, Gav and Holty, but in terms of the day-to-day running I was on my own, working 15-hour shifts just as I used to. For years I'd delegated everything except buying the stock – now, once again, I was doing everything.

I had to organise the computer now and my skills were so shit I couldn't even switch the machine on. I'd employed people to set up the website and other people to run it for me. I was so inept I had to get written instructions from Holty. He looked after the computer in those days and, initially, I was glad I'd been able to retain him. But then he was offered another job so I had to let him go.

'I don't have to take it,' he said. 'I can stick around if you want me to.'

'Take it,' I told him. 'I want to keep you on because we've been friends for years and you've been brilliant. But I can't give you any guarantees so maybe you ought to take the job – just show me how to work the computer.'

He did and it was literal:

1) Press power button on bottom right-hand corner and hold for three seconds.

2) Release button and wait for computer to boot up.

I was that bad, honestly. I don't think I slept for days. I locked myself away and taught myself how to use it properly. A week later Holty was gone and I was modifying the database. Gavin took a job doing some double-glazing work but still restored for me on Saturday and Sunday. I was on my own but I could work the computer, and I'd remembered how Rob Wilding had done so much business on eBay. I started shoving masses of stock through there and gradually the money started coming in. I managed to keep the kids in school at £3,600 – per child – per term and I don't know how I did it.

Things improved, but there was something wrong and it went way deeper than just the business. It was like those panic attacks when they first happened, I didn't know what was up or how to fix it until one day in the warehouse a month into the recession.

The week after I bought the cabinet and urn from Peter, I travelled to Oxford to film the classic car show. It's a series I do with my mate Paul Cowland called *Salvage Hunters Classic Cars* that came about due to the success of my first TV series where my passion for cars became apparent. It's about finding cars from all eras that need restoration. We source them, fix them up so they look brand new, then reveal them later before they're sold on to, hopefully, very happy buyers.

We did some work in Banbury before revealing a 1970 Fiat 500 that had been a complete wreck when we bought it. It got even worse when we took the paint off as that had been holding the bodywork together. I restyled everything, changing the colour, the wheels, engine and gearbox, as well as the interior. It was transformed into a thing of beauty and, when we revealed it, we brought whole sections of Oxford city centre to a standstill. Hundreds of people stopped to stare at the deep black paint and chrome bumpers; it's one of the best transformations we've ever done. Not only that, it was the best day of filming I can remember. There was something really cool about driving this Modernist gem of a car around such a beautiful old city where the architecture dated back to the fourteenth century. People loved it; they were chatting away, queuing up to take pictures with us and the car. It was fantastic.

There's a lot less pressure on me when I do that show because I don't have to go out and find lots of different things; I'm basically being paid to do my hobby. During the last series I bought a pre-airflow Mark I Ford Cortina manufactured in 1964 that came from South Africa. There's no rust. It's never had any welding or bodywork done, and, right now, it's in Dundee waiting to be collected. Paul's fun to work with, a man with a lifelong passion for cars; what he doesn't know would fit on a match-head. Really, we're just dicking around with old cars, but there's nothing better than seeing a beaten-up hunk of metal recreated as something both functional and beautiful. A rolling work of art (as I like to say); so it was with the Fiat 500.

We'd bought an MGA a few months back and that resto-ration was designed to create something an enthusiast could rally. It was painted duck-egg blue with a silver roof. I had to go to Telford to source some seats and had located a com-pany called Cobra. That name intrigued me, because it evoked the car created by the late great Carroll Shelby, a racing driver and entrepreneur with a heart condition, who took on the might of Ferrari and beat them. It was something I brought up when I met Mark Dunsford, the managing director.

'So, tell me,' I said. 'The name Cobra, is that anything to do with AC?'

'Oh, yes,' he said. 'Very much so.'

He was a nice guy; a lot of fun and I could tell his work-force really liked him. He told me how his grandfather,

Len, was one of the foremost coach trimmers in the country back in the early 1960s. Working for AC Cars out of Thames Ditton, he built seats for racing cars driven by such luminaries as Jim Clark and Stirling Moss. Rising to be the company's head coach trimmer, Len was there when Shelby showed up to see if it was possible to squeeze a seven-litre Ford V8 into an AC Ace. With a few modifications it could be done; the subsequent car they created was bound for Le Mans and the rest is history. The first AC Cobra was completed in 1962 and tested on what was the brand-new M1 motorway. The story goes that in the early hours of a Sunday morning they took the car out to see how fast it would go and it was absolutely blistering. A combination of raw Ford power and an aluminium body, it's alleged it was down to that test that there's a 70mph speed limit on UK motorways.

Mark's dad served a short and eventful apprenticeship at AC working with his father. But he messed about so much Len told him he would have to leave before he got him the sack. He lasted six months then left for a job with Moto-Lita steering wheels. With a background in coach trimming, he tried to persuade the owners that they should make after-market car seats but they said there was no money in it. Mark's dad wasn't convinced, so he started his own company from a shed in Camberley and got an order for 50 seats from Gordon Spice Engineering. Pretty soon business was booming so he moved to Telford because it was a

New Town with an offer of free rent and rates. Every seat is hand-made and, 40 years later, the company is the biggest competitor to Recaro. They make all the seats you see in the dugouts at Premier League football grounds, having originally been approached by Manchester United. The headrest is removable so whenever they change sponsor a whole new seat doesn't have to be manufactured.

Mark took me upstairs, where he had a couple of seats for me to look at. 'This is the department we call Brushing and Bagging,' he said. 'The final inspection where each seat is brushed and cleaned; it's where my mum used to work, before she moved to the sales office.'

He showed me a bucket-style seat with a headrest that looked a little modern but was the sort of thing I wanted. It had a dog-tooth check, which he told me was the original Porsche pattern.

'Really?' I said. 'I'm just restoring a right-hand-drive 1968 911 and was tempted to go that way, but we've got the original seats so we'll stick with them.'

I took a good look at the other two seats, both variations on a theme, and could see the quality. They weren't quite right, though. I knew the kind of thing I wanted and would recognise it when I saw it. 'I like these,' I said. 'But they're too modern. I need something that feels MGA.'

'Right,' Mark said. 'No problem.'

'I want it to look classic but racy. We're selling the car and I think the kind of person who buys it will be at – let's call it – our time of life, so they need to be able to get in and out without it being a problem.'

'OK,' he said. 'Something that looks old but still gives lateral support without being too tall at the side so you don't give the driver a hernia.'

He came up with a classic-styled bucket seat that looked like it might've been made for a Cobra from the 1960s. It was low at the sides while still hugging the body and didn't have a headrest. I ummed and ahed about whether to opt for one, as Mark said they could figure something out if we thought it was necessary. I wasn't sure; it was more about the overall look of the seat and it had to be in keeping with the age of the car. In the end I plumped for the seats as they were and we decided to fit them with a Whillans-style four-piece rally harness. After that it was a question of the fabric, and Mark showed me just about every style and colour you could imagine. I chose a grey/blue plaid that would fit the age of the car and complement the bodywork properly.

'So, how much are we talking?' I asked him.

'We need to doctor the seats a little so they fit the car. With that and the fabric – four hundred pounds apiece.'

A pair of bespoke seats with full harness and trim for 800 quid, I'd shake on that all day. 'Great,' I said. 'When can I have them?'

A good chunk of what I've written about so far involves filming, but being on television was never something I envisioned. That said, a few years before *Salvage Hunters* started, I made a brief appearance on a BBC show called *The Reclaimers*. It was a one-off, though, not a career choice. The opportunity came up, and I took it so I could get some more exposure for my salvage business.

I certainly needed exposure in 2008: the recession was still hitting me hard, and I was determined to get back to where I'd been previously. That day in the warehouse I mentioned before was a watershed, and not just for the business. I needed something to get us rocking and rolling again, but I also needed something for me personally. I had to think of a way to inspire people and I had to express who I was within the trade, because I had no true identity, but I also wanted to be free from the shackles of convention and conformity.

For two days I couldn't sleep, I had this thing in my head about changing things up, and a day or so later I went to the photography area of the warehouse and stared at the white wall we used for the background. I had to change it. I don't know why, but I had to do something fresh, and black has always been my colour. I had some Farrow & Ball paint so I got a brush and painted the wall matt black. I liked it, a different look; now I had to set something against it. I dug out some 1970s Pagwood stacking chairs and placed two side by side on the floor then threw the rest on top. Taking a step back, I considered the jumbled result and thought it looked great, so I ought to take a photograph. The only camera I had was 40 quid's worth of digital from Tesco on a tripod I found in a skip, but it worked and I began snapping pictures.

After uploading them to the website, I went home and grabbed some sleep, and by the time I got up in the morning the chairs had sold. I thought, Fucking hell, how did that happen? I realised then that it wasn't just for sale purposes I'd done this; it was for me. I had to show people what Drew Pritchard was all about in terms of the antiques business. For so long this trade has been staid and steady, dominated by posh people looking to maximise their profit. It had never been that way for me. It was a love of things that were rusty or weathered, old and forgotten: it was beauty, poetry; even music. I'm a massive music fan and told you I grew up with Madness, The Specials and The Who. I have everything Paul Weller ever recorded from his time with The Jam, through the Style Council to his solo career. He's an icon, an innovator, a 'mod' in the truest sense of the word; and I totally identified with his music because he's an artist who really did go his own way. As far as I was concerned, the business that chose me wasn't staid and steady, it was rock 'n' roll. What I did with that pile of chairs was release all the frustration and tension; the *having to conform* to what everyone else in the antiques business thought. But I didn't think that way. I'd initially been grabbed by old cars floating in the air. I sought chairs that generations of people had sat on, desktops worn to the grain by elbows. No item was static, they all had a life of their own. In that moment of matt-black paint and Pagwood chairs, everything I'd been told, everything I'd learned about the antiques business was tossed out the window. I thought, Fuck it, I'm going to do this my way.

The next thing I did was get a chain and hang it from the ceiling. Then I found a really good Edwardian club armchair I'd bought and strung it up on the chain. I grabbed a bench and put Enzo on one end and took a photo. That's what went on the website, a shot of my dog that showed only a tiny section of the bench I was selling. I went from idea to idea and put all the pictures on the site and it felt like a dam had burst inside me. I'd allowed myself to become stymied by the recession and how this business was supposed to work, when all along I should have been doing it my way. I moved on to a mahogany chest of drawers that I turned three-quarter-ways on then pulled out half the drawers and dumped a couple of toy cars inside so they looked like they were falling out. I was invigorated, an artistic vent had opened and I was no longer defined by convention. The effect was incredible. I was doing what I wanted and I no longer gave a shit what anyone else was thinking.

I didn't know it then, but I'd announced myself to the upper echelons of the antiques business, and I mean people I really respected. As I was driving home one night not long after those first images hit the site, the phone rang and it was Alex MacArthur from Rye telling me that what I was doing was brilliant. Alex is one of the dealers I really look up to and I didn't know what to say. The top of the tree, the best of the best in her chosen field. I'm like: *Are you kidding me? Alex MacArthur thinks what I did with the website is brilliant.*

We had a really in-depth conversation but I was driving and distracted so I stopped in a lay-by just down the road from the garden centre. Half an hour later I said goodbye and was about to pull back onto the road when the phone rang again.

'Hello?' I said, not recognising the number.

'Oh, hi.' An American accent. 'Is that Drew?'

'Yes.'

'This is Ray Azoulay from Obsolete in California.'

Fuck me. First Alex and now Ray Azoulay. These were people at the top of their game. I remember thinking, What the hell is going on? In the space of just a few minutes two major influences on my life in terms of antiques were on the phone. I was tongue-tied as Ray echoed everything Alex had said. 'You're doing great things, I'm really impressed.'

The hairs were prickling the back of my neck. 'Thank you,' I said. 'Thank you very much. You have no idea what that means to me.'

I'd grabbed his attention working with 40 quid's worth of Tesco camera and, as the weeks went by, he started buying stuff off me. Alex bought too, but not like Ray. He bought masses and shipped it out to California.

Looking back to those dark days of the recession, it's hard to believe I'm where I am today. Things could have gone completely pear-shaped but that moment in the studio changed everything. My outlook was fresh, I was no longer a slave to conformity. I felt free to really express myself and had found another way to reach people. I still had the garden centre but the whole operation was much leaner and I realised I preferred it that way. That didn't change the fact I was determined to get back to where I'd been, though, and in order to do that I had to rely on experience. In just under a month I'd gone from assets of three and a half million to minus-80 grand in my buying account. I'd put the properties up for sale so I could pay off my debts and I was trying to shift the inventory. By the end of that month I was back to £60,000 in the black and I was kicking on. Everything bar the garden centre had been sold (the long-winded deal in Llandudno not-withstanding). I'd kept the chapel and changed the way our stock was displayed on the website. I'd had a Eureka moment with Alex and Ray, and there was light at the end of the tunnel. But then there was more scaremongering on telly about double- and triple-dip recession and business fell off again.

I was struggling through when one Saturday afternoon I sat down at the desk in the Glan Conwy warehouse to leaf through the *Antiques Gazette*. It's the bible of the trade and I've been reading it for 20 years. Right at the back, I spotted an advert no more than 4cm square that was edged in black.

> **Are you a man with a van who drives around salvage yards and demolition sites collecting architectural salvage and antiques?**

It had been placed by a TV production company with a number to call and, as soon as I read it, I knew I fitted the bill exactly. I'd already done *The Reclaimers* and remembered the director telling me I was pretty good and should do more TV if the opportunity ever presented itself. I'd enjoyed it; a piece of piss. I didn't have to impress anybody. I was just talking to camera about something I love.

I cut the advert out and pinned it on the blackboard but it was Saturday and nobody would be at the production company, so I decided to give them a ring on Monday. Of course, things cropped up, it went out of my mind and the advert remained on the board for weeks. Business picked up a little and I was out and about, then a dealer showed up at the warehouse.

'Drew,' he said, as he opened his wallet and brought out a copy of the same advert, 'have you seen this?'

I pointed to the one pinned on my board. 'Saw it weeks ago,' I said. 'Never got around to phoning.'

'You should. "A man with a van" – that's you.'

Again, it was Saturday, but after he left, I did pick up the phone. There was no one in the office to take the call so I left a message on the answer machine. When I got home, I told Rebecca and she said, if anything came of it, she'd back me.

I went into work on Monday and the production company was on the phone right away. 'Mr Pritchard,' the woman said, 'we'd like to film with you. I want to send a crew. Is tomorrow OK?'

'Sure,' I said. 'OK.'

They turned up early and I did a bit to camera outside the warehouse and they left again. Christmas came and went, then early in the new year I got a call from the office asking me if I would be interested in a series to be broadcast on the History Channel. Of course, I would; but nothing happened and I just carried on with my business. A year went by and it was the following Christmas Eve before I heard anything from the production company. I'd shut the shop and was on my way home when the phone rang.

'Hi, Drew. This is Izzy from the production company in London. Sorry it's been so long since we were in touch, but that's how it is in the television business. Anyway, I'm calling with good news. Congratulations, you've got a ten-part series with the History Channel.'

I wasn't in the least bit surprised. Despite the amount of time that had passed, when the film crew left, everything had felt right and I knew I was going to get it.

We started filming the following March. The money wasn't much but it would only take a few months and I thought it would be the easiest bit of cash I'd ever earn. As it turned out, it was actually the hardest work I'd done in years and that was down to the travelling. Until you're on the road day after day, week after week, you've no idea how gruelling it can be. Today we only do one location a day, but back then we did two or three with 100, sometimes 200 miles in between.

My motivation wasn't what you might think; it had nothing to do with being on TV. I've never wanted to be famous, but for me this was the best advertising I could get for my business. Hopefully, people would see the show and ring up to sell me stuff that I could restore and then sell on at a decent profit. This had already happened after I did *The Reclaimers* and I had no interest other than generating stock for the website. It never crossed my mind that the show might be successful enough to become an income stream in its own right, it was just another way of buying antiques.

So, I thought it was going to be a piece of piss, but I admit I was pretty nervous that first day. It's important to point out that this wasn't the production company that make the show today, but its predecessor and they're no longer in existence. But, that aside, it wasn't just one bit to camera; it was an entire series and everyone was much more experienced than me. It was a bit of a stuttered start in actual fact, and almost got derailed completely due to a clash of ideas between me and the director. The production company sent over a young, Swedish director who'd already had a worldwide hit. He was experienced and I wasn't and we took an instant dislike to each other.

Back then I was still driving an eight-year-old, beaten-to-shit E300 Mercedes estate which had done 180,000 miles. With rust in every corner it looked like the *Bismarck*. The director told me we'd rehearse how the first call was going to play out and he wanted a piece to camera in the car with me.

'We'll pretend you're travelling to the destination,' he said. 'Discuss how you're going to play it and what you're going to say.'

'Alright,' I said. 'Let's go.'

So, we jumped in the car with me driving and John Nutter, the cameraman, in the passenger seat. The director was in the back along with Simon Jolly. We got onto the A55 and had driven about two miles when the director starts in with the set-up.

'OK, Drew,' he said in a really annoying nasal accent. 'We're going to see this woman. Tell me how you're going to rip her off.'

'What?' I looked in the mirror at him.

'I want you to go in there and absolutely smash the price. I want you to rip her off.'

'No chance,' I said. 'I'm not going to do that.'

'What're you talking about?'

'I don't rip people off.'

'Yeah, but this is TV.'

'I don't care. It's not what I do.'

He took a moment to absorb that then told me that, whether I liked it or not, that was the show.

'Bollocks to that,' I said. 'I'm not going to rip people off, that's not what I do.' I was adamant and the guy was beginning to bug me. 'This might be your show and I don't mind taking direction, but I've got a business to run. How am I going to do that if all they see is me ripping people off on TV?'

'Yeah, but the contract.'

'Fuck the contract. I didn't sign up to rip people off.'

He would not let up, kept going on and on about this and that until I swivelled round in the seat and jabbed a finger at him. 'Listen, mate,' I said. 'You're missing the point if you think I'm going to rip people off. You can tell me until you're blue in the face, but I'm not going to do it. There's no fucking way.'

He just stared at me with his mouth open.

'I mean it. You keep on like this I'm going to lose my rag and things will really kick off, I promise you.'

He was smiling, shaking his head as if I was stupid and just didn't understand what he wanted. That was it. I really lost my shit and pulled over into a lay-by. I was in his face, telling him if this was what they thought the show was going to be about it was news to me. Clearly, they had no idea who I was, so I told him I'd spent years building up a reputation and I wasn't going to blow it all for the sake of TV. Whatever nerves I'd had were gone and I was fuming.

I'd had enough so I drove back to the yard in silence. I'd never come across anyone like this guy before and he'd never come across anyone like me. When we got there, I jumped out of the car, went around to open his door and was about to drag him out, but then a little bit of sense kicked in. I had a contract and I'm a professional. TV presenters don't go around fighting directors, but there was no way I was going to work with him.

'You see that building,' I said, pointing to the warehouse. 'That belongs to me and you're not allowed in there, OK? You've got me all wrong and you need to listen because, if you step inside, I won't be responsible for what happens to you.'

I had to get a handle on my temper and the only way I could do that was if he was nowhere near me. I had a contract with the production company but that contract wasn't with the director. The company would have to sort this out or just forget the whole thing and I knew they wouldn't do that because the channel was expecting a series. As far as I was concerned, that wouldn't include this director and I refused to let him inside the building. Looking back now, the crew must've been wondering what the hell they'd got themselves into. The director got on the phone to London and a little while later Philip Whelan, the series producer, called to tell me I had to do what I'd been asked to do. I told him straight, I don't rip people off and this was over if that's what they wanted me to do. We had a chat, then he said he'd come down and sort things out so I put down the phone, not quite sure what to expect when he got there.

Immediately he jumped in a car and arrived at the warehouse a few hours later. He calmed things down and the two of us tried to work out a way we could get on with the series. I was adamant I wasn't going to rip anyone off and I could not work with someone who wanted me to do that, so the director flew back to Sweden. I'd made it clear to Philip that the show would only work if I was allowed to do it my way. It had to be exactly as it was when I was buying without a film crew; open, honest and no bullshit. He agreed and we all took a couple of days for the dust to settle, then the crew came back with another director. His name was Mark and I don't know if he was expecting some firebrand Welshman but he was pretty wary around me. But only to begin with: I'd calmed down, and the bottom line was the show had to work, so we agreed to make that happen.

With Mark at the helm we made a plan of how things would play out with me just being me. After that we hit the road, heading for our first location in Lancaster. I was excited now, again a little nervous, but all that disappeared when we arrived at a real shit-hole of a hotel and that set me right back again. I could feel a panic attack coming on and it was made worse when we went to a steakhouse for dinner and the food was absolutely appalling. So much for bloody TV. This was 48 hours after the shit with the first director; the hotel was crap, we couldn't eat the food and I was so stressed I shut myself in my room. I had to deal with the panic attack and had learned how to do that, but it wasn't easy. Somehow, I managed to get myself together, but was plagued by attacks the entire shoot. I had one every single day. I could've set my watch by them. Philip could see how stressed I was, and he was able to defuse the situation completely. He's a very funny guy, always cracking jokes, and that lightened the atmosphere considerably.

'Drew,' he said, 'just be yourself. If you know about something and you're talking, just keep going. We want to know what you know. We'll cut what we don't need for the show.' That was the best piece of TV advice I've ever been given. It chilled me out and a relationship was forged that I still respect today. He became someone I trusted and I think he understands more about why people watch a particular programme than anyone else I know.

The next day we were filming with a dealer called Golly and I found a couple of really interesting items. It was a lot of fun and we got through it pretty unscathed. On the second day of filming we were in Blackpool at the Illuminations warehouse, so we stayed in a hotel attached to the Pleasure Beach. Gavin came up to join me and there was another film crew staying in the hotel, some of whom Philip knew. They came over for a drink and the director was a bit pissed by the time she talked to me. 'Whatever you do, don't turn into an arsehole,' she slurred at me.

'I've got no intention of turning into an arsehole.'

'Well, don't.' She poked a finger in my chest. 'That's what happens in this business.'

'I won't,' I promised, and she went off to annoy someone else.

'What was all that about?' Gavin said.

'She was telling me not to become an arsehole.'

'It's a bit late for that,' he told me.

CHAPTER 8

BUGATTIS AND BEETLES

Whenever I'm buying, no matter how far I am from Conwy, I always try to make it home at the end of the day. It's only if I'm in Scotland or the southeastern corner of Kent, maybe, that I stay in a hotel. When we filmed the first TV series, however, I lived out of a suitcase for four months solid and home seemed a long way away.

I only say this because, ten years later, I've spent my life in hotel rooms and it was the last thing I ever expected. There's so much glamour attached to TV, but the bit you see is only a small part of what actually happens. So far, we've made 250-plus shows and I'm just about to sign up for another two and a half years. I've still got 18 months of my existing contract to run, so that's another four years with four different hotels per week, which adds up to about 750. I'm not moaning, far from it; I'm only too aware what the TV series has done for the profile of my business and I wouldn't have it any other way. All I'm trying to say is that life on the road making show after show isn't necessarily all it's cracked up to be. It's draining, repetitive, you don't see your family and that can cause all sorts of problems. For example, at two o'clock this morning, I was pacing another strange room trying to breathe my way through a heart palpitation. I got there eventually, but it's debilitating to wake up covered in sweat with your heart racing in unfamiliar and often uncomfortable surroundings. I don't ask much of a hotel – a decent bed, a shower that works and reasonable food – but one of the things I've learned over the past ten years is that, in Britain, we do terrible hotels really well.

We began filming the first series on 22 March 2010 and it lasted 16 weeks. I still had a business to run and spent my evenings uploading stock onto the website. When we were finished and the crew went home, I returned to buying on my own as I'd done for years. Nothing changed but the show was yet to air; when it did, I was hoping I'd get people on the phone wanting to sell me stuff I wouldn't otherwise have come across. The schedule had been much tougher than I thought it would be, but I was happy that I'd dug my heels in and was able to do it my way.

I'm sure it's apparent by now that I have huge respect for the antiques trade as an entity in itself and every part of what I do has to maintain that authenticity. So long as the edit was done in the right way the viewers should see the reality and that might draw more people to the business. So much of what is shown on television doesn't portray this trade properly. Most programmes bear no resemblance to how it works: people don't walk into an antique shop and look at an item the dealer has up for £100 and offer £15. I've seen that on the telly and, after a bit of back and forth, the dealer accepts the £15. That just does not happen and it creates a false impression of what we do. I know for a fact that the second filming stops a runner is there with the other £85 to give to the dealer. What's the point of a 'reality' show if it's not going to deal with reality?

More often than not, the dealers you see are only posing as such; they're auctioneers and there's a fundamental difference between an auctioneer and an antique dealer. Auctioneers sell on behalf of clients and their knowledge of any particular item is generally nowhere near as extensive. Take that Regency Waterfall bookcase Peter Whipps bought that was catalogued as a kitchen dresser. As far as I'm concerned, many of the TV shows about the antiques trade do nothing but damage the industry. They do not represent me and they do not represent any of the people I know and respect.

Proper antique dealers have spent a lifetime learning their craft in exactly the same way as a great chef or musician. If you watch Marco Pierre White or Rick Stein, for example, when they're cooking and talking about food, you get the real deal. Equally, if you watch me talking about antiques, you get the real deal, just as you do with someone like Rupert Maas on *Antiques Roadshow* when he's describing a painting. It's obvious he knows exactly what he's talking about and has a genuine passion for it. To use food as an analogy, I equate the daytime antiques programmes with pot noodles. It's still food, it's still got multiple ingredients; you have to do something with it before you can actually eat it, but it's not food you want to eat. It's not real, it's fake, and that's how I feel about those programmes. They are 'boil-in-the-bag' television. That may sound harsh but think of it this way: if there was a programme out there that denigrated lawyers in the way some of those shows denigrate what I do, they'd be sued to high heaven. How can anyone take this business and all the nuances that go with it, not to mention the decades it takes to learn and be any good, then bring it down to that level? Being an antique dealer is like learning to play an instrument, you get to a point where you can do it but you have to keep on doing it and doing it if you want to get to any kind of serious level.

As far as our show was concerned, I'd done the first series, we were waiting for it to air and I was looking forward to seeing it. When I signed up, the production company were in talks with the History Channel where it was thought they'd put it on immediately before *American Pickers*. That was great, I'd seen *American Pickers* and, although it revolved around the same kind of subject, it was a very different show to the one we did. Just before the programme went out, however, I had a phone call from the production company telling me it wasn't going to be History now, but

Discovery. They had a new channel called Quest and the show would be broadcast on that platform instead. I wasn't sure about that; I'd never heard of Quest; it didn't bode well and I was beginning to dread what I might see. A TV show is all about the edit and we film hours and hours of material, most of which doesn't get anywhere near what is actually broadcast. The wrong cut here or there can completely alter the perception of a transaction and that's what I began to fear.

I needn't have worried; when the show finally aired what I saw was the real me. There on the screen was the bloke I'd been determined to get across and the one *I* recognised, let alone anyone else. They hadn't dicked about: what Philip Whelan had promised would be the show *was* the show and I was delighted with the result. He'd done right by me when he could've cut it any way he fancied and made me look like the kind of rip-off merchant the original director had wanted. He didn't do that and he has my lasting respect for honouring everything I was trying to achieve.

It was all very positive and the fact that it wasn't shown on the History Channel no longer mattered to me. Nothing really happened though; there was no great change in my life, people didn't start recognising me on the street; nobody stopped to shake my hand or tell me they thought I was rubbish. But what I'd hoped would happen did. Immediately, people started ringing in with stuff they wanted to sell and I had access to a whole new marketplace. I'd achieved my objective: made sure they saw the real me, and it was clear I didn't rip anyone off. 'Drew Pritchard': what you see is what you get, no frills, no bullshit, just someone who loves finding antiques to restore and sell on to someone else who will appreciate them. This is the best job in the world and you have to respect it. It's multifaceted and multilayered; it's interesting, beautiful, dangerous, rude and crude all at the same time. You immerse yourself to the point where you think you've found your place, then it changes completely and that happens again and again. What you thought was definitive isn't. There's another facet and another; you're learning something every day.

So, business kicked on, we were smashing it again, but I didn't hear anything from anyone to do with the TV show. I didn't think about it, it hadn't been a career choice; I was already doing what I wanted and, if that one series was it, I'd done what I set out to do. Then one day (when I least expected it) the phone rang and it was the production company telling me they wanted to do another series. That was great: I knew what I was doing now and they'd proved they were happy to do it my way. The only question was whether we were going to keep the same personnel. During the first series it had largely been me and a mate called Julian who worked with me, together with a few episodes where Gavin came along. By the time I got the call to do the second series, however, Julian was no longer working for me. The company asked me if there was anyone else I could think of who might fulfil the role, and get back to them as soon as possible.

It wasn't hard. All I had to do was ask myself who I'd want to hang out with in the cab of a van day after day for months on end, while staying in crap hotels. The answer was simple – T. I thought he might be up for it, because he'd worked as a roadie for years and could cope with all the travelling. He's my friend and he's rounded; interesting and a little bit punk like me. As soon as we knew Julian was out of the frame, I got on the phone to him.

'Hello, mate, how've you been?'

'I'm alright, keeping busy, you know.'

'How busy?'

'What do you mean?'

'I mean, what're you doing for the next three months?'

'I don't know yet, but I'm not going on that shit programme of yours.'

Typical T, I hadn't expected anything less. I told him it would be a laugh; we'd have a good crack and the company would give him at least what he was earning now.

'They'll pay your hotel bills, give us lunch and you'll get fifteen pounds in per diems a day.'

'Go on then,' he said.

T's been with me on the show ever since and the ease with which we work together is mirrored on the classic car show I do with Paul. When he first started out, Paul won't mind me saying he was what we call a tiny bit 'TV', but I knew what I was about and what was wanted. By then I'd been doing my show for nine years and it only took a couple of days to knock off the edges. I'd known Paul for a few years and his real persona is just like me and T. Paul is a pro, and once he relaxed into being himself, it was absolutely brilliant, easy, really good TV.

That show is about finding, fixing and selling classic cars, but with all things automotive there's 'classic' and then there's 'classic', and Paul and I don't always agree. That was the case with the Honda we bought the other day. A black two-door CRX VTEC that Paul had heard about from a guy with a warehouse on a farm outside Reading. We'd been in Banbury the day before so it wasn't very far to travel. We already had 20 projects going on, and the MGA was well on the way to its reveal, having been fitted with the seats from Cobra. I'd loved the Fiat 500 of course, and we had a beast of a Volvo 850 that needed a new headliner, the material that lines the inside of the roof. That was all good stuff, but this VTEC Paul was raving about was hardly a rolling work of art and didn't come anywhere near the classic brief for me. VTEC means Variable Valve Timing & Lift Electronic Control, and it's all about the profile of the camshaft that allows more air into the cylinders at higher speed, which generates more horsepower and hence you go quicker.

'A Honda?' I said. 'They haven't been around long enough to be a classic.'

'Of course they have. They made a pickup called a T360 in 1963.'

'So, what year's this hatchback?'

'Early nineties, it's the VTEC that makes it classic. The engine, it's very clever.'

I'm not as anal about the internal combustion engine as Paul, but I know enough to understand VTEC and, yes, it's clever, but clever doesn't make it classic.

'A 911 is a classic,' I said, as we drove through country lanes towards the location. '1960s short wheelbase or the 993; that's a fantastically engineered piece of design right up there with the T35.'

'Bugatti again, Jesus, you never stop banging on about them, do you?'

'That's because the man who designed them was a genius. His whole family were like that, amazing people, visionaries. There's never been another car like the Bugatti. I can't afford one but I've got bits and pieces, including the original sign from the factory.'

'So, where's the sign now?' Paul said as we turned.

'Hanging on the door of my living room in Conwy.'

A few years back, Rob Bellis, a dealer pal of mine from Llangollen, called me.

'Drew,' he said, 'you're not going to believe it, but I've found the original sign from the gates of the Bugatti factory in Molsheim.'

'Really?' I said, not even trying to hide the sarcasm.

'Yeah, really. I mean it. It's the actual sign.'

'How do you know?'

'I've got an old photograph that was taken outside the gates and the sign's right there and it's the same one. I'm telling you, this is the original.'

Rob's no bullshitter, and after ten years in the business his knowledge is pretty solid. He's a really good guy, I like him a lot and there was something in the tone of his voice that made me sit up and take notice. If he was right then this was something very special, and I trusted his judgement enough to make the drive to Llangollen. Like any good dealer, he didn't tell me where he got the sign, only that he was sure it was something I'd want to take a look at.

When I got to his place, he brought out the sign and I took a really close look and it seemed authentic to me. It was around 45cm wide and had the right patination; I knew there were copies out there, I'd seen them before and had been thinking that this might be one, but the moment I clapped eyes on it I was certain. That ain't a copy, I said to myself. That's exactly what Rob said it was on the phone. The wear was right, the colour and quality. The size, scale, fit and finish; just the general feeling told me this was the real deal. It was confirmed when he brought out the old photograph taken outside the factory gates where the sign that I held in my hands right then was hanging for all to see.

'What do you want for it?' I asked him.

'Four hundred quid.'

'Yep, I'll have it. Thank you.'

I've had that sign for a few years now, one of those dis-coveries that's up there with the gadroon wine cooler and the 'Voyage to Vinland' stained-glass windows. It was on my mind because I'd just come back from the Goodwood Revival where there were Bugattis all over the place. In a rare moment of downtime, I'd taken off to attend the motoring festival that started in 1998, 50 years after the 9th Duke of Richmond opened the racetrack in West Sussex. It's two and a half miles of tarmac designed for both cars and motor-bikes, and the revival recreates a period when Goodwood rivalled Silverstone as Britain's number-one motor racing venue. What's really cool is the fact that during the three days of the festival no modern vehicles are allowed inside the perimeter apart from ambulances and rescue trucks.

I wandered among short-wheelbase 911s and Bugat-tis. There weren't just T35s, but Type 55s, as well as a two-seater Atalante coupé with rear mudguards that swamped the wheels a bit like an Indian motorcycle. Long in the bonnet and short in the boot, it's such an amazing piece of design that was produced between 1934 and 1940. What I love about those cars is the fact that they're not just hidden away under a dust sheet in an air-conditioned garage while the value goes up; the people who buy them use them and race them.

To see so many in the flesh had all my senses tingling. One caught my eye that was covered in dead flies and dirt kicked up by a 1,000-mile drive from the French Riviera. It had luggage bags hanging off the sides in a real tribute to a bygone era. It was right-hand drive and I spent a good half-hour chatting to the owner. He shared my view that this was the highest form of art. Strong and light, designed with a simple yet absolute purpose, it stirs the same emotions today that I first felt when I was eight years old in Glan Conwy. Nothing has changed except my level of knowledge and experience.

It's raw, brutal, honest; and I'm convinced that without Ettore Bugatti we would never have seen the Modernist movement. To me, all aspects of design have some connection and that's a complex idea to try to get across, especially when you're not the most educated guy out there. But I talk about links in a chain and for me Ettore holds a special place in that chain. Modernism isn't just art, it's philosophical and cultural, and spawned trends that reverberated across the planet.

Goodwood is where I went to race my VW Beetle after it was finally completed back in 2010. It was something I'd always wanted to do, as racing is in the Pritchard blood. My grandfather John on my father's side was a bit of a wheelsman, and when he died I went through one of his old wallets and found more speeding tickets than you could imagine.

He even had one for riding a pushbike, can you believe that? He got fined for speeding on a bicycle. My father thinks he's a wheelsman, my brother too, as well as me; we all think we're a bit better than we probably are. When I was 19, I was sat in the pub with T and a lad called Crofty, all of us car-mad, and I told them I was going to design a black 1950s Beetle with BRMs, 356 brakes and a straight-cut gearbox linked to a 2.2-litre engine. I was going to hill-climb, sprint and circuit race … and 20 years later, I did.

Business was good, we were into the second TV series and I'd started to make a few quid. I was busy as hell but found the time I needed to think about racing and start making a few important contacts. They're everything in the racing world, and I made many of mine through a very good friend called Stewart Imber, who has become almost a father figure to me. I'd read about him when I was 17 in a classic sports car magazine: he had a farm in Hertfordshire with the most incredible collection of Mercedes Benz from the 1950s and 60s. There was an SE cabriolet, a coupé and a 600 series, as well as a Fintail and Ponton that he was racing. It seemed to me he'd bought the most beautiful cars at just the right time and in exactly the right condition, and that struck a chord with me.

Over 20 years later I arranged for us to film with Stewart at his farm in Hertfordshire. I'd wanted to meet him since I read the article and we clicked right away. Since then I've filmed with him maybe six or seven times and he invited me to a classic car race meeting. I jumped at the chance; it had always been an ambition to race classic cars but I never thought I'd have the opportunity.

Now I just might be able to do so. I had the money and the contacts I'd need to build the car I'd talked about all those years ago, but it was no small undertaking. Typical me, I wasn't about to get a Mini and start at the bottom to work my way up; I was going to build something that nobody had ever done before. At that time there was no competitive VW Beetle on the British historic racing scene. One project had been started by the managing director of Porsche UK but he couldn't get it finished. Since then there have been a few, and right now a young guy is building a car, but then there was nothing and I believed I could not only do it, but also win the 'Touring Greats' class. Stewart was a great help. He's been part of the Goodwood Revival since day one, together with Julius Thurgood, who runs the Historic Racing Drivers Club. I joined the HRDC and later I set about having the car built. Then the bills started coming in. My God, is it expensive to build a race car. I'd had no idea just how much I was going to spend if I wanted to do it properly, but I'd collated a team of individuals to do the work, having sourced the car in the southern states of America.

A '58 Deluxe in black that had been lovingly restored arrived in the UK and we immediately stripped out every mechanical part, taking it back to a shell. From that moment I was bleeding cash. I remember telling the lads to ring me every time they spent five grand, and in one week alone they rang three times. That's the nature of race cars, you have to have passion and you have to have the money. It took 18 months to complete and, once it was done, we wangled our way into the Goodwood members meeting. Prior to that Paul Cowland helped me get my racing licence in a hot Subaru, a process where you get the initial licence, which effectively gives you a set of 'L' plates, then you complete a dozen or so races before you're fully qualified.

Everything seemed to be falling into place and, the day before the members meeting, I was sitting on the start line in my full-spec 200bhp screaming VW Beetle about to do my test day. I remember thinking, How the fuck did I get here? Since then there's been a seven-page article in *Octane* magazine on the car, written by David Lillywhite. I've made loads of great contacts, and next year I'm commentating on the Monaco Historic Grand Prix for the second time with Marino Franchitti (younger brother of three-time Indy 500 winner Dario). He's spent a career racing sports cars and GTs, and I'm really looking forward to going. That morning at Goodwood, though, it was freezing cold but the car looked the absolute nuts and was getting loads of attention. I was completely blown away when Ivan Dutton, a Bugatti restorer who specialises in T35s, told me it was the best-prepared car in the paddock.

That was the test day, and in the members meeting that followed we were assigned a professional racing driver to take the car for qualifying. A professional and a privateer, those are the rules; he or she gets grid position and you do the race on Sunday. When we knew who our driver was going to be, I took him to one side and pointed out where he had to be careful because the car could get sideways and he just looked at me.

'It's a car,' he said, and walked away.

OK, I thought, this guy knows what he's doing so I'll just let him get on with it. With his knowledge and skill, I'd get my lap position and tomorrow it would be my turn.

For the previous 18 months we had poured blood, sweat and tears as well as a ridiculous amount of money into creating this car specifically to race at Goodwood. Together with a mechanic called Andy, the engine had been built by Ian Clark of Wolfsburg Performance Services and it was an absolute work of art. Ian's dad was a clockmaker who taught him that art, which he perfected and later started messing about with Volkswagens and Porsches. His skill as an engineer is beyond comparison; he works on his own from a farm in Lincolnshire and people fly their cars in from America so he can tune them.

Ian, Andy and I were in the pits with the rest of the team watching the monitor as the professional driver went out to get us our qualifying position. This was a very special moment, a VW Beetle racing at Goodwood; it had never been done before, and tomorrow I would achieve all that I'd told T and Crofty I would two decades previously. It was magical, we were surrounded by well-wishers who echoed Ivan Dutton's belief that ours was the best car out there. Our turn came and we watched with bated breath as the driver went from 13th to 3rd on the grid. It was amazing, the car was like a rocket and we were riveted to the monitor. It was going superbly well, better than any of us could've expected. Then, on the last corner, we saw the car scream into view with smoke pouring out the back. I remember thinking, What the fuck, then the driver pulled into the pits and told us it just went on him; he had no idea what happened. It wasn't his problem, it was ours, and when Ian checked underneath, he found a con rod had pierced the bottom of the engine case, smashing it to pieces.

That was it. The weekend was over. There would be no race tomorrow and it hit me like a ton of bricks. To say I was gutted would be the understatement of the year. It was so bad I couldn't actually be near anyone else; I just wandered off on my own. For the next three hours it felt as though my world had collapsed, I just could not believe it. So much effort, so much time, so much of my soul had gone into the project, it was beyond anything I'd ever done before. Finally, someone came to find me and, when I went back to the pits, they told me there was something I had to see. We had a GoPro camera inside the car and it had captured what actually happened. I watched the lap and saw the speedo hitting 80mph in fourth gear, then the driver changed down – but instead of hitting third he put the car into first. There was no way the drivetrain could cope with that, and it smashed everything to pieces. I can't begin to explain quite how low I felt, and the fault was nothing to do with me or the engineering crew – it was purely down to driver error but there was nothing we could do because he could not be held accountable.

As we pulled up onto a gravel road that led to a large industrial warehouse outside Reading, the guys selling the Honda were waiting and my first reaction astonished me. I like cars. I love cars, but I've never had such a visceral dislike for any vehicle ever. At first glance I hated it and it didn't get any better when we got out to take a closer look. As I walked around the thing, I thought it was the biggest pile of shit I'd ever seen. Paul, on the other hand, was purring. 'It's really cool, Drew,' he kept telling me.

'No,' I said. 'It's not. It's horrible.'

I love Paul, hopefully we'll be friends for the rest of my life, but when it comes to what's cool, he really hasn't got a clue. The car was just dreadful. 'I know it goes like stink,' I said. 'And I know the VTEC is an amazingly clever engine, but I really don't care. It's shit. Everything about the way it looks is awful.' I was shaking my head. 'I want nothing to do with this car; nothing.'

The wonderful thing about the car show is that from day one they let me do whatever I wanted. If I loved something, I could wax lyrical all day, and if I hated something I could say so. I hated this. It was absolute crap and I didn't pull any punches. Fortunately, the guys who were selling it were there on behalf of the owner so I wasn't hurting anyone's feelings.

'Paul,' I went on, 'the whole point of our show is motoring icons. We're trying to find cars that stir something in people.'

'Right,' he said. 'Like the VTEC engine, and that's what makes this iconic.'

'No. It doesn't,' I said. 'What's iconic is a Mark I, eight-valve Golf GTI or a Mini Cooper.'

'Or a Dodge Challenger,' he suggested.

'Exactly, that's an icon that goes all the way back to *Vanishing Point*. It stirs something deep in people and that doesn't happen with a little black Honda that might drive like a race car but wouldn't be seen dead on my drive. We're not looking for converts here. This show appeals to people who are already hooked; they'll laugh at us when they see this. It's not a car, it's an appliance like an iron or a toaster. It's got all the charm of a verruca.'

It was all to no avail. Paul was buying this shitty little car even if we had to pay the full eight grand they were asking. He thought it was the best thing since sliced bread but I just couldn't see it. The truth is he and I agree on three makes of car without question: Porsche, Volkswagen and Subaru. After that it's a grey area.

'Paul,' I said, 'he's asking eight grand, which is eight grand too much. I'd rather set fire to my feet than part with the money. That car is a blot on the landscape; if someone gave me a JCB I'd happily dig a hole and bury it.'

'So, you don't like it then,' he said.

'Get that, did you? I fucking hate it.'

'It's a landmark,' he said. 'A Honda CRX double-overhead cam SiR.'

'Which translates as Stupid Irrelevant Rubbish.'

'I reckon he'll take seven and a half,' he said. 'Wheels off, brakes changed and the suspension. I think we can get eleven grand, no problem.'

Oh sure, I thought. Hopefully it'll catch fire in the meantime.

Most of the time we're on the same page, though, so I suppose we can agree to disagree on what is and is not a 'classic'.

CHAPTER 9

THE POWER TO CREATE AND RESHAPE

Once filming for the day was over, Paul went home while I headed for yet another hotel where I had to get as much stuff uploaded onto the website as possible. After dumping my bag, I started work with the 6:00pm deadline rapidly approaching. Every Wednesday and Friday we send an electronic mailshot to 60,000 subscribers alerting them to the very latest wallop of stock I've put on the website. It has to be out by 6:00pm and it was already 5:40. That gave me just 20 minutes and there were some really nice items I wanted people to see. It's one of the moments in the week I really enjoy because it generates immediate interest. The stuff I was uploading was eclectic and that's been our signature since I had the moment with the Pagwood chairs and Tesco camera. The new items had only just been bought and restored, and it's a challenge to add real quality twice a week.

Equally, the timing is critical. I can't be late because by five past six we start getting emails from interested parties.

With just ten minutes to go I had a Welsh blanket uploaded as well as an abstract painting and two wooden lay figures, which was a great mix, but there were still another couple of items to go. When it comes to antiques, I'm a purist but also a bit of a magpie. I don't care if something retails for 15 grand or 150 quid so long as I'd be happy to own it.

The lay figures were interesting, not the best I've bought but still very good, and there was a kind of naivety in the manufacture that really appealed to me. I've got a passion for these articulated figures and I have three at home, one I bought by chance that's right up there with the Roman wine cooler in terms of just how special it is to me. The one I was uploading now I'd bought on the way back from Goodwood, having also stopped on the way down. Just as we got to West Sussex, in fact, I'd spotted a sign at the side of the road that said ANTIQUES and it turned out to be quite a find. I picked up some wonderful little Christopher Dresser brass pouring jugs for a couple of quid apiece as well as a whole stack of other stuff. I love Dresser; he was an interesting guy and considered to be a really important independent designer back in the nineteenth century. Born in Glasgow in 1834, he died in Mulhouse in the Alsace region, 70 years later. Mulhouse was both a city and artists' commune, and Dresser was both a designer and a design theorist (which is the philosophy behind design). He was a big part of the Aesthetic movement that focused on art and literature rather than the political themes of the time.

So, I already had a carload of stuff when we stopped for the night in Oxfordshire. On Monday morning we drove through the Cotswolds, where I always do well, and called on various dealers. By the time I was done, I'd spent more than 20 grand and had so much stuff I had to send a van down to ship it back to Conwy. I wasn't finished yet, though; there was one more place to stop and that was Baggott's in Stow-on-the-Wold. It has to be the most 'antique' of any antique shop in Britain and the owner is old-school like you wouldn't believe. He's incredibly knowledgeable, with a fabulous stock, and I call about four times a year. I rarely buy anything, but this time I spotted a lay figure in the window with a price tag of £1,800 and knew immediately I wanted to buy it. Inside, the owner and I got talking and it turned out he was a big fan of the show, though I had no idea. I mentioned the lay figure and told him I was interested; it was just a case of how much I'd have to pay. It was unusual in that it was pine not a hardwood, and it was nineteenth century not eighteenth, and it's eighteenth-century figures I collect. He said he could do it for £1,500 but I managed to get it down to £1,300. Since then it had been photographed and there was every chance I'd double my money. If it had been eighteenth century or earlier, I'd have kept it. Not forever, nothing is forever, but there's a time to buy and a time to sell and it's up to me to make that decision.

In 34 years of buying lay figures I've only come across three that were worth keeping and I've still got all of them. The best I've ever found was at a museum of rural life in Kent, which was a brilliant call where the curator was great and we had a right old laugh all day. They had a school-house there, so they sat me and T down and brought in this old schoolmaster to shout at us and I was reminded of my childhood in Glan Conwy. We bought a few bits and pieces, bric-a-brac mostly, nothing that had stood out specifically but that was OK. The crew had a few last general-view shots to take care of and I wasn't required, so I had a wander around on my own. Not all areas of the museum were actually open and I took the opportunity to check out a couple of olde-worlde shops that we hadn't been into. I wasn't looking for anything; I wasn't even really thinking about anything, it was just a moment of downtime.

As far as I could see the shops had become storage sheds for the kind of tat museums don't really want but always get given anyway. You know the kind of thing: potato peelers and garden rakes, old stools that aren't very old, generally any old shit somebody wants to get rid of. Inside they were dark and dusty and one was partitioned by a counter. You never know what you might find in the recesses, though, so I stuck my head over just to be nosey.

On the other side, lying on the floor covered in shit, was the single best lay figure I'd ever seen. About a metre tall, it was eighteenth century and just the kind of thing I collected. As I picked it up, I had to disengage a ravenous woodworm that was literally eating its head. Now I really was excited. This was English, with a trace of original paint on its face; the most enigmatic, sculptural, artistic and magical lay figure I'd ever come across. I knew I had to have it.

So, I went to track down the curator and showed him the figure. 'I just found this in one of your old shops,' I said. 'It was lying on the floor in a pile of dirt being eaten by woodworm. Is there any chance you'd sell it?'

Before he even opened his mouth, his expression told me everything. 'I can't,' he said. 'It was gifted to the museum.'

Shit, I thought. I'm not going to be able to get it. I couldn't believe it; gifted and yet lying in a pile of crap on the floor of a shop that was not even an exhibit. It would rot back there – if I hadn't come along the woodworm would have devoured it. I was gutted, but I understood that, if something has been given to the museum, the custodians can't just up and sell it.

'Alright,' I said. 'I get that, but if anything changes, I'll give you three thousand pounds for it.'

The man looked absolutely gobsmacked. 'Three thousand?'

'Right here. Right now, if you're prepared to sell it.'

'I can't,' he said. 'I'd like to, but I just can't. We'll clean it up and store it properly.'

'Don't clean it,' I told him. 'If I bought it, I'd want it just as it is, only without the woodworm. You need to keep that away or it'll be completely ruined.' Reluctantly, I handed the lay figure to him and departed.

I remember telling T just how pissed off I was at not being able to get it. It happens, though; you don't always get what you want, and so it was with that lay figure. But you move on and I did, and pretty much forgot about it. Then, two and a half years later, the phone rang.

'Mr Pritchard?'

'Yes?'

'This is the curator from the museum.'

Museum? I thought. What museum?

'Down in Kent, you were here a couple of years ago and we talked about a lay figure. You said you'd pay three thousand pounds for it; I don't know if you remember?'

'I do,' I said.

'Does the offer still stand?'

'Of course.'

'It's yours then, if you want it.'

Again, it was one of those moments you really never expect. I didn't think the figure would ever be for sale, but it was, and it's worth every penny of the £3,000, because I get a huge amount of pleasure every time I look at it.

*

CHAPTER 9

The symmetry of a top-drawer lay figure reflects the level of industry and dedication, not to mention talent, it requires to become a great artist, and it is great artists who create different artistic movements. The way those movements tie in with other aspects of our culture has always held a huge fascination for me. For example, just as the Aesthetic movement was all about art and literature, so the term Modernism reflects the trends of another period in European history. If you look at the origins, you'll find references to the 'power of human beings to create, improve and reshape'.

Discovering and understanding the various artistic movements was part of the learning process that began when I was a spotty little kid. Some forty years later, I can't look at anything without thinking a thousand different thoughts and making a thousand different decisions, because my mind has become attuned to viewing things in a particular fashion. I instantly know why something was made in a specific way and where the manufacturer's influences came from. Instinctively, I understand what they were trying to say. The best antiques are pure, with the artist or artisan having travelled one particular road without veering from it one iota. It's both passionate and slavish. They have this idea in their heart that they want to show to you and that's exactly what you see. If you look at pieces from Art Nouveau or pure Aestheticism, English Regency, you get where the artist was and what they were trying to achieve in a deep, almost spiritual way. You amass more and more knowledge and the learning curve just keeps climbing. It affects every aspect of your life and you begin to understand why you think and feel in a certain way. One thing leads to another and you start to recognise how you've developed as a person and the influences that have shaped your own particular journey. Take music, for example; it's been a huge part of my life and has influenced my appreciation of this business that harks back to the origins of Modernism.

I already said that from a very young age I was obsessed with ska, two-tone and the whole mod scene. The 40th anniversary of the film *Quadrophenia* was marked with a cast reunion on TV on 21 September 2019. When I saw it advertised, it set me thinking about the way music has influenced my career right from the very beginning. I'm in love with scooters; I've got lots of them and for me it's Vespa rather than Lambretta. Scooters represent an explosive period in British culture that hit a second wave in the late 1970s. It was all about mod, a fashion statement and musical movement that has echoes harking back to the attitude displayed by the man I consider to be the greatest British artist ever: J.M.W. Turner. He was part of the Romantic movement, but anticipated both the French Impressionists and Modernism because he sought to break down conventional methods of representation; to my mind, that's exactly what the mod revival of the 1970s accomplished.

You're probably thinking that it's quite a leap from Turner to The Who, but the way I learned to see things has enabled me to understand the passage of time and how one cultural or architectural movement links to another. 2-Tone Records was a label started by Jerry Dammers of The Specials that attempted to break down the barriers and racial tensions that existed in Britain during the years of Margaret Thatcher. Bits of the original Jamaican ska from the 1950s were mixed with punk rock and new wave and became a massive part of the Anti-Nazi League that grew up in urban centres all over the country. It was music and clothing: The Specials, Selector, The Beat, and a slightly edgier connotation from The Jam. Those bands were at the forefront of something that echoed the breaking down of traditional barriers that began with the Modernist movement. Rather than paintings and buildings, it was an audible and visual reflection of a change on the streets of Britain that I became part of as I grew up in North Wales. It was Crombie coats, Dr Marten boots and three-button suits. It was the two-tone bowling shoes The Jam brought into fashion when they first hit the scene with their single 'In the City'. I was only seven at the time but the energy of the whole thing was like being punched in the face. The very first record I ever bought was the 1980 'Too Much Too Young' EP from The Specials that I still have today.

It's a constant reminder of a time when my learning curve was growing exponentially and music culture was part of it. Mods, rockers, skinheads and soul boys; none of that tribalism exists any more but for me it was part of a surge of expression. Without the music there wouldn't have been such an interest in scooters, and they've become as big a part of my life as VWs and Porsches. The whole scene was incredibly British and I don't think it could've happened anywhere else; but the scooters, the coffee and fashion were all from Italy and that excited me.

Long ago I decided that, when the time is right, I'll knock all this on the head and fuck off to southern Italy. I'll buy a little house somewhere I can sit with a dog and watch the world go by while I dabble in antiques, because it's something I'll do until they box me up and burn me. I intend to slow the pace, listen to music and use a classic Vespa to get around on.

The Vespa – the word is Italian for 'wasp' – predates the first Lambretta, and the first model was on the market in 1946. It was made by Piaggio, who were an aircraft manufacturer before and during the Second World War. When the fighting ended, Enrico Piaggio, the son of the company's founder, realised Italians needed a cheap and 'modern' form of transportation. Two years earlier two of the company's top engineers had designed a motorbike with bodywork that fully enclosed the drivetrain. It had a tall central section and a prominent headlamp that made it look like a duck, so they called it 'Paperino', which I'm told means 'Donald Duck' in Italian. It wasn't bad, but Enrico thought they could do better and the first fully fledged Vespa was launched in 1946 with sales of a couple of thousand. That steadily increased, and in 1950 they sold 60,000 of them. The model was given a massive fillip when Audrey Hepburn rode pillion to Gregory Peck in the 1953 film *Roman Holiday* and the Vespa quickly became the go-to ride for Hollywood superstars.

I was into scooters the first time I ever saw one. We always had loads of old motorbikes around our house and it was the age and patina that got me. My father had over thirty and knew everything about pre and post-war models, the flat-tanks and Nortons, BSAs, etc. One of his mates, a guy called Smutty, used to race the Isle of Man TT and another good friend made leathers – Alan Kershaw, he's still around; I bumped into him the other day and he's still got all the old patterns including the one for Barry Sheene's race leathers.

My father used to come across motorbikes in the most unlikely of places. I remember going with him in his old minivan to a house with an old barn somewhere above Llanrwst and that's when I first learned the art of 'knocking', which I used later when me and Clive Holland went car hunting. It's a term in the antiques trade for when you're driving around and get a feel for a particular place then knock on the door with a story ready. It would usually go something like this:

'Hello, my name's Drew and I'm here to see
Mr Roberts about the old motorbikes you've got for
sale in the barn.'

'Mr who?'

'Roberts.'

A shake of the head. 'No, there's no Mr Roberts
here, I'm afraid, but we do have an old motorbike if
you want to look at it.'

That's exactly what my father did and invariably he'd find
some gem that had been locked away for years. When
we got to the house above Llanrwst, my father 'knocked'
and, yes, there were motorbikes and we were welcome to
take a look at them. The owner of the house led us to a
shed/workshop attached to the barn but I couldn't see any
motorbikes anywhere. He had a workbench about waist-
height and 60cm deep running all the way around the shed,
and underneath the bench were two motorbikes. I didn't
see them because he'd taken the wheels off so he could sit
them on the frames and slide them in, so they didn't look
like motorbikes. But there they were, and I had no idea just
how amazing a find this was until I was a lot older. Those
two bikes were Brough Superiors, which is what Lawrence
of Arabia was riding when he got killed on a road near Bov-
ington. I don't know what my father paid for them, but he
did some kind of deal and they were added to his collection.
He must've had half a dozen Manx Nortons as well as other

classic race bikes, including a trials Greeves that I burned my leg on when we went to a barbecue at Rowen in the Conwy Valley.

Motorbikes were everywhere, and me and my brother Guy would mess about with them, even though we were told to stay away in case one fell on us or something. There was one in particular that we had to steer clear of but never did, a late 1950s or early 60s Ducati race bike where the stand had been worn into a very sharp point. That was due to the standing starts where the rider would run to his bike and slide it off the stand before jumping on and bump-starting it. By the time that bike was added to my father's collection, the stand had been so badly worn it was little more than a spike. Me and Guy had been dicking about when we'd been specifically told not to, then I went off to do something else, leaving him with the Ducati.

The next thing I knew, bedlam broke out with my mum screaming, my father shouting and everyone running around because my brother was pinned to the floor by the stand on that Ducati. He'd been rocking it from side to side, lifting the spike off the ground, only for it to come down with all the weight of the bike on top of his foot and go right through it to pin him to the floor. Before I knew what was happening, I was in the back of my parents' Mark I Cortina estate with a black, blue and purple bathroom towel wrapped around my brother's foot and blood everywhere. We went to hospital and Guy was alright. Not long after, though, Smutty was killed racing at the TT and my mum told my father he had to get rid of his collection. He put them on the open market and a German collector came over and bought the whole lot to exhibit in a museum.

Maybe what happened back then is why bikes never held quite the same attraction for me as motor scooters. Simple and yet beautiful, functional and fun; the perfect combination of two-wheeled design and engineering. They were clean and stylish, suited to the city and easy to ride, with no exposed drivetrain to get oil on your snappy trousers. I think that was partially why they appealed to mods: a way of zipping through town in your best clobber without having to get changed after. As a statement the scooter went hand in glove with the music and clothing. It's personified in *Quadrophenia* where the first wave is explored in a uniquely British way. We didn't create Modernism and we didn't create Brutalism either. We didn't actually create punk rock either – Iggy Pop did that about three years before it exploded – but the mods were British through and through.

I was too young to own one but I wanted to be part of mod, i.e. modern culture. It was obvious to me when I was eight or nine and my mum took me to Blackpool with the youth club she used to run at Llandudno Junction. Already I was into The Specials and Madness and I used to cycle five miles to Llandudno along the main road to look for the kind of sunglasses Chas Smash wore, but could never find them. When I went to Blackpool, it was on a coach full of skinheads in donkey jackets and Dr Martens. We arrived at the Pleasure Beach fairground and everywhere I looked it was more skinheads as well as mods in suits and fishtail parkas. Everywhere I looked it was scooters. It was another Eureka moment, coming not long after I'd seen the cars at Piccadilly Woods, and I remember thinking, Oh my God, that's me. That's me done. That's where I want to be.

It grew and grew and that's when my dad painted the mural on the wall of my bedroom. I was already into ska, but I started listening to The Jam and the music got under my skin to the point that it stayed with me all through the 1980s. When I was older, Oasis came along with a British vibe that for me echoed The Kinks and Small Faces. It was something Blur tried to emulate but never quite managed. I know the Gallagher lads can be idiots at times, but no matter what you think about them, their music has an iconic feel and, as time goes on, I think they'll sit in the same uniquely 'British' space as The Kinks and Paul Weller. The music Oasis played reflected their roots on a council estate that I experienced for a while myself when I was growing up. It never leaves you. It doesn't matter where you live now or how much money you've made; the raw reality of a British council estate is inescapable. Oasis embraced that. It was a case of 'That's who we are and we're not going to apologise to anyone.' It's exactly the same with me and it was true of the entire mod movement.

Music and fashion, and the cultural changes they release, are as important to me as antiques, and it's in the Vespa that those two strands of my life come together. As far as I'm concerned, it will always be the best form of two-wheeled transport, personified in the 1959 GS. A perfect piece of engineering and design, its beauty is in its simplicity. There are no frills to a 150cc 1959 GS. Unfortunately, I don't own one, but my mate Dave has one that's absolutely beautiful. Just as the T35 is the most beautiful Bugatti and the 911 the best Porsche, the 1959 Vespa is the icon of all motor scooters. I have the 1960 model, and bought it because it was untouched, completely original and, although it just misses that purity of design, it's still a work of art. It's the best in my collection and five are GS Vespas. The Lambretta is actually better to ride; it's lower with a longer wheelbase, and Phil Daniels' character is riding one in *Quadrophenia*, but it's the Vespa GS that gets the iconic mention from The Who.

My 1960 model is painted cream and I bought it from a contact I still deal with in Sicily who specialises in hunting down classic scooters. An American girl called Lee, she called me on the phone ten years ago, then sent pictures and I just fell in love with it. I didn't need to fly out, I could tell how good it was and I parted with £4,000 in order to buy it. All my mates told me I was mental – four grand for a GS that wasn't the '59. What the fuck was I doing?

I knew exactly what I was doing; that scooter has more than doubled its value, although I've backed off buying them these past few years as I've had to really concentrate on the business. I'll probably get back into it again, but for now that 1960 GS is not only the stand-out scooter, it's also part of my personal heritage.

CHAPTER 10

HOME AND AWAY

Over the past couple of years, I've been keen to really spread my wings in the search for a yet more varied range of antiques. It's a global business with no physical boundaries and the show is broadcast all over the world, so it's important to get out there where people can see what we do first-hand.

Filming abroad is a mammoth undertaking with the largest crew we ever assemble. There's Rob the director, Sean and Steve on the main cameras, Simon the sound man, our assistant producer Olly, as well as Carl who operates another camera, our runner Conor and Dan Trelford, the series producer. Hugely experienced and someone I have the utmost respect for, Dan was a fan of the show who wrote to the production company telling them he wanted to get involved, then he elevated what we do to a whole new level altogether. A man who can spot real talent, he's seen it in various members of the crew and helped them expand their careers.

Being on the road overseas is different to being on the road here, with an opportunity to meet new people and see new places. The trips are great fun and any issues that have arisen from the pressures of filming in the UK seem to get blown away. The only downside is that we have to get a lot done in a short space of time and travel vast distances. Imagine being in a rock band on tour without all the drugs and sex, but lots of beer and crap food, and you'll have an idea what we get up to.

It means I'm nowhere near the showroom, though, and sometimes it bothers me. I wonder what I'm doing. I mean, I used to be an antique dealer (and quite a good one) but what am I now, exactly? Am I still a dealer or am I someone who appears on TV? I've tried to combine the two and work very hard to keep a consistent flow of quality stock, as I have nine people on the payroll to consider. But the fact I'm no longer 'dealing face to face with clients' bothers me. The business is fine, we're smashing it again, but it's a continual balancing act and requires a lot of headspace and energy. The upside is that trying to perpetually do two things at once keeps me sharp, and sharp is where I need to be. That said, I really miss the day-to-day mixing with customers. You know the sort of thing; people walking into the shop for a bit of a look around.

'Hiya, mate. What you got? Oh, yeah. I'll have that.' Bosh, on to the next one.

There's a rhythm to dealing that's very important. Come March 2020, we'll have been doing the show for ten years and it's what I spend most of my time working on. Back when we first started, we'd film for three months and it would take a week to get back into the swing of dealing, but then I'd have six months solid on that before another round of filming. As the show became more successful, however, the intervals between filming grew less and the time it took to get back into the selling side of the business got much longer. I'm talking about the ebb and flow of the thing, and the more that rhythm is broken the harder it is to get back into. It's one of the many variables of the antiques trade that's quite difficult to get across, but it's something I've always been conscious of. I liken it to a cantering horse, constant movement at a speed that's both comfortable and manageable. If the stride is broken, it's hard to get it back and that's what I've had to give up in order to make the TV show. I still have all the buzz that comes with buying because that's what I'm doing day-in, day-out; it's the selling side, the interaction with regular customers, I miss out on.

Because no two items are ever the same, there's a freshness to dealing that gets you out of bed every morning, but there's also the network of clients you've hopefully built a rapport with. Sometimes the customers who come into the shop are first-timers, but more often than not they're people you've dealt with before, and if you're clever you'll make sure you know the kind of thing they're in to. If you don't have what they want, you can plant a seed by letting them know what's coming in. If you've looked after them properly and gauged them right, they'll want to be the first to view and you're halfway to the deal already. That's how it works, a garden of clients and dealers you nurture in order to keep the business growing.

This whole trade is a series of relationships. It's an affinity with regular clients who might be members of the public or other dealers, auctioneers or interior designers (decorators, as they call themselves). As I've already said, my problem with so many of the shows about antiques is that they make it all about the sale, the bargain; and it really isn't like that. It takes years to get to the level of dealing where you've established those all-important relationships and it's something I strive to maintain despite the demands of TV.

You can't have it all, though, can you? I suppose the flipside of losing some of that rhythm is that I'm doing something else now as regards the antiques trade. As I said before, I never wanted to be a TV person because I've never sought the fame or notoriety that tends to go with it. What I wanted to do was get across my passion for antiques and bring more and more people into the business. You may not like me, you may not like the show, but I guarantee someone has walked into your shop or auction house because they watched us on TV. That expands the business and can only be good for all of us. These days I'm not just working for myself, but every antique dealer in the country.

Hopefully, what I do is a good influence on the trade and, from what most proper dealers tell me, it seems to be. I've been told that the show is authentic and I know it has inspired lots of people. But, remember: just because you buy a silly hat and open a shop doesn't make you an antique dealer. That takes years, and the important thing is to establish your own identity. What you shouldn't do is copy me. I've lost count of the websites that have sprung up that are a straight copy of mine; some are so close they look like they've been cut and pasted. If you are going to create a business, you need it to be individual.

I did that years ago when I had my moment in the warehouse with the Tesco camera. Since then my business has evolved and it's been helped by the TV show, but there's a downside to that because being in the public eye is crap. Honestly, it's shit. There are very few upsides. Everybody thinks you're an arsehole and I get so much flak, it's ridiculous. When someone watches an episode of the show, it's important to remember that it's a mere 46 minutes of my life and I shouldn't be judged by that alone. I make money, that's why I'm in business; but it's my money we spend and it's my risk and I have no spare minutes to call my own. Sometimes that can be really debilitating and it only adds to the panic attacks. It can get too much, particularly when you've just got back from a long trip away and you're in the car again facing a six-hour schlepp to another hotel. You've barely had time to toss your dirty clothes in the washing machine before you're back on the road.

The fact I do so much travelling is pretty ironic actually, given that when I was a kid my mum used to tell people

I hated going anywhere. If you put me in a car for half an hour, I was sick and had a headache. My eczema would flare up, I'd be tired and moaning and want to go home. Fortunately, that's not the case any more, particularly when it comes to travelling abroad. We're a team on the road, out of our comfort zone, and we all muck in. It's a period of bonding. If you ever bump into us, you'll soon see there are no 'stars' and no airs and graces. If I ever got too big for my boots, the entire crew would very soon let me know. There's a sense of togetherness that's forged not only from what we're trying to achieve, but from the fun we have as we're doing it.

The first foreign trip we made was to Norway back in 2012 and it was a great success, though an expensive place to stay as well as to buy antiques. Since then we've been to Spain and France, as well as a few other places, but we were yet to go to any of the old Soviet Bloc countries, so when a trip to Hungary in September 2019 was mentioned I jumped at the chance, as I'd never been there before. I love to travel, because it both improves my eye and expands my knowledge, and I was interested to see what might be about from the Soviet era. The night before, me and Simon Jolly stayed in a Manchester hotel then left for the airport in plenty of time to make the plane, only for Simon (who was born and bred in the city) to direct me the wrong way. I was travelling light as I always do. Generally, I'll prepare my bag then go through it and toss out everything that's not totally essential.

Hand luggage suffices for a couple of weeks; I've learned it's the best way to go. Despite heavy traffic and heading in the wrong direction, we made the plane and the buzz was in full swing when we landed in Budapest and hooked up with the lads who had flown from London. We got the hire vans packed with all the gear and I was really up for exploring.

Budapest is a fantastic city situated in the north of the country and bisected by the River Danube, with a population close to a couple of million. The sprawl goes on and on, covering over two hundred square miles of Gothic buildings and Soviet-era apartments. It's chock-full of cultural and historical icons; the Museum of Fine Arts, the Hungarian National Museum, the Franz Liszt Academy of Music and the State Opera House. But we weren't going to any of those, we were headed for a massive flea market to which no self-respecting dealer would venture alone.

Our assistant producer Olly had already been out for a recce and organised a fabulous secessionist hotel in the city centre that used to be a public bath house. He's brilliant, the kind of guy you can parachute in and know he's going to come up with something really special. I refer to him as our resident lunatic: boundless energy, but a huge amount of nous and enthusiasm, as well as a love of the antiques business, so that makes my job a lot easier. He had organised the first couple of calls and spoken to potential contributors, as well as doing the groundwork on where we'd stay. It's not a simple process, and obviously too big of a financial risk to wing it entirely, so Olly flies in armed with a small camera and a backpack and gets chatting to people. From those conversations he figures out where to go and who to talk to. That information is relayed back to the office and the trip set up with the kind of rough parameters that allow us to improvise still if we want to.

With a great hotel lined up for the first couple of nights, the crew was really happy and we were all happier still when we found a bar within spitting distance that charged 50p for a pint of lager.

'Fantastic, Olly,' I said when he came down to find me. 'This is really great, you've outdone yourself.'

'Glad you like it,' he said. 'The flea market tomorrow should be eventful.'

I had my notes on the table and was scribbling a couple of things down and he looked a little quizzical. 'What're you doing?' he asked me.

'Writing a book.'

'Really? T said as much. I thought he was joking.'

'No, it's true. I was working on it on the plane.'

'What's it about?'

'Me and the antiques business.'

'Is T in it?'

'We all are, Olly,' I told him.

He grabbed his pint and necked a mouthful. 'Well, if they want to know what I do, tell them I spend most of the time herding a flock of shit-faced ducklings.'

That's not a bad description, but it's much more than that really. With a bit of research already done, I know we'll get great stuff for the show and really enjoy doing it. We work very hard and the hours are long, but we also play hard and our tight-knit group is all the stronger for it. We make the most of every call and, hopefully, that comes across to the viewer. The camaraderie between us seems to rub off on the people we meet, and we met a lot of fans of the show this time, which is avidly watched in Hungary. I'm always amazed at how many people have seen it evolve from the early days when it was just me and T piling into places full of damp and dust to the expansive series it is today.

Having dumped our stuff and partaken of the odd 50p pint, we went out to eat at a restaurant Olly had scoped, where we were introduced to our fixer, Lazlo. Apparently, that's the most common name for a boy in Hungary, and I discovered that our Lazlo was a journalist who worked for the national press and was really into antiques. A big guy in his fifties with no hair and a handlebar moustache, he'd arranged to take us to the Ecseri flea market, which takes place every day in Budapest. But, as I said, it's not the kind of place any of us would venture alone, and there were dark-eyed gangsters all over the place looking to scam us. The moment Sean rocked up with the camera, one of them asked for his passport, telling him he couldn't get in without it. Sean's too long in the tooth for that kind of crap so he just shouldered the camera, looked the bloke in the eye and went on through.

I've been to one or two flea markets in my time, but this place was a world away from anything I'd ever experienced. Part indoors and part out, it was filthy, smelly, and the main warehouse looked as though it had been there since the 1920s. Most of the shops or stalls were about the size of three toilet cubicles and there were hundreds of them all over. Outside, people parked knackered old cars side by side and sold from their open boots.

Everywhere I went I was accosted by a gang of Romanians who were prattling in broken English. They'd obviously seen the show and kept grabbing me and trying to get me to go with them. 'Drew,' they said, 'come and look. We've got great stuff. Come and see.' They were pretty insistent and they didn't seem to be with ones we had to avoid, so I tagged along with them. The cameras weren't on yet, Sean was still setting up, but this place had such an atmosphere I dropped into dealer mould right away.

All my instincts kicked in when I spotted a painting that was 150cm tall by 60cm wide that just said something to me. Oil on canvas, it was a life-size portrait of a young boy dressed in a blue coat and white collar, holding a rifle. There was something in his face, the expression both angelic and yet a hint of devilment. A kid from Eastern Europe with a rifle, it wouldn't have been unusual for the period. Dated 1918, it was good, I mean really good, and I knew I had to do a deal right then otherwise I would lose it. I was still being mobbed by the Romanians but managed to speak to the vendor and asked him how much he wanted.

'Five hundred euros,' he told me.

No, I thought; that's not happening. I like it but not that much. 'How about three?'

He shook his head and held up four fingers.

'Four? Alright, I can do four hundred, but I can't take it now, you have to hold it for me because we need to film this for the television show.' He didn't understand at first but I managed to get the message across with hand signals and the international language of cash. Fair play to the guy, he did hold the painting and, when we came back, I bought it on camera. That's something we never like to do because the whole point of the show is to be natural, and the things I buy are the things I see when the camera is rolling, but I knew I'd lose this if we waited.

That first purchase set the tone for the whole of the day. We wandered from cubicle to cubicle and some were pretty good and others not so. A lot of the dealers were selling Soviet-era furniture, which has its own mid-century, morbid style, but we had to wade through lots of junk and crap in order to find the real items of interest. One guy operating out of a tiny shop looked like Father Christmas, but spoke good English. He'd seen the show and beckoned me over.

'Drew,' he said, 'come over here. Come on. There's something I want to show you.'

He looked like an interesting guy and his collection seemed pretty eclectic. The first thing that struck me was an eighteenth-century Japanese tapestry hanging on the back wall; the quality of the workmanship was fantastic. But it was rotten, so bad it looked as though it would fall apart at any moment. I loved it, it was a wonderful thing, but I doubted it would make it as far as the van without disintegrating completely. He clearly had a terrific eye, though, and knew his subject.

This was great, a real dealer in this sea of cubicles. I took a closer look at what else he had going on apart from that amazing tapestry. There were lots of great things but none that set the hairs standing on the back of my neck until I spotted a tiny drawing. Graphite on paper, it was an image of a man's head and that man was clearly going through some horrendous torment. No more than 15cm by 8cm in the frame, I flipped it over and on the back were stickers from all the galleries the picture had been through in the early part of the century, which meant it had already been recognised by the trade as quality. Fab, I thought, that's brilliant. I looked closely at the picture again, and only then did I realise there wasn't a curved line in the drawing. The artist had taken a pencil and used it to create tiny individual strokes that made up the image of a tortured soul who just spoke to me. There wasn't a line out of place, the skill quite incredible; it reminded me of how Picasso used a single line to draw an entire fighting bull.

'How much do you want?' I asked the guy.

'Sixty euros.'

Without thinking I offered 50 and we shook hands. It was ridiculous, the dealer in me had kicked in to get the price even lower when this was one of the best pieces of art that had ever crossed my path. It was one of those really rare moments that come along just a few times in your life … and I've seen some incredible artworks, believe me. I was angry with myself for dicking about on the price; this was insanely good and I'd offered ten euros less than the paltry amount he was already asking. I knew I had to make recompense because the drawing stirred something in my soul and it was one that would hang on my wall at home. A man in absolute despair; someone at the end of their tether completely. I knew there wasn't a person alive who could not identify with him and I asked the dealer how long he'd had it.

'Oh, ages,' he said. 'I bought it months ago.'

I couldn't believe it. In any art gallery anywhere in the world this drawing would fetch a couple of thousand easy. I was feeling really bad but the deal had been done, so there was nothing I could do except buy something I didn't want and make sure I paid full price for it. Spotting a nondescript load of other paintings the guy was selling as a job lot, I asked him how much he wanted.

'A hundred and fifty euros.'

'I'll have them,' I said. 'Thank you.'

I left his shop with the best piece of art I'd seen in a while and we hadn't even got started. It was a great omen and I was beginning to think Hungary might be as good a foreign trip as we'd covered. As soon as we moved on, I was grabbed by another bloke who'd been following us around all morning. He told me he was a massive fan of the show and I had to come and see his emporium. As we cut through the crowd, he started telling me about some of the things he'd found down the years and how he'd been in the market every day since he was 13 years old.

Instead of trading from one cubicle, he had about ten spread all over Ecseri. We walked into the largest and I immediately spotted a really good painting of a guy in his sixties. Clearly Hungarian in origin, the dealer told me it was one half of a framed pair and dug out the other. Standing side by side they showed an older man and his extremely stern-looking wife: 'Mr and Mrs Wagner'. Painted in the early nineteenth century, I liked them a lot but he wanted 150 euros, so I had a think about it. While I was doing that, I turned around and saw a collection of what looked like doll's furniture displayed on the back of the door. There was a sofa and two tubular steel chairs in red, as well as a circular coffee table. At first glance it looked like something a kid might play with, but I knew it wasn't doll's furniture. Another of those incredible moments, the second in a matter of minutes. I was looking at a collection of salesman's models created by a designer called Jindrich

Halabala in 1950s Czechoslovakia. I knew his work; one of the pre-eminent Eastern European designers of the time, he was born in 1903 and spent his early years as a cabinet maker before enrolling in the state-owned woodworking school in 1920. In his early twenties he joined the firm UP and became their development manager, where he was able to bring his belief that furniture should be functional, modular and mobile to the fore, and pioneered mass-market industrial furniture in Czechoslovakia.

This stuff was rare, very rare. To find Halabala models in a flea market was pretty much unheard of. Back in the day, the salesman couldn't throw a sofa in the back of their NSU and travel the country; instead they were issued with scale models and this was a complete set of living-room furniture. I bought that and I bought Mr and Mrs Wagner.

All day we went from shop to shop, and T was as surprised by the quality of the stuff as I was. The market just seemed to go on and on; there were literally hundreds of stalls and shops; no sooner did we get to the end of one row there was another and another. It wasn't long before I had a fantastic painting of some Russian ladies called 'The Gleaners'. It wasn't the kind of thing I'd seen before so I parted with 150 euros. By the end of the day I'd bought a dozen paintings, as well as the Halabala models and this amazing bronze of a man in the style of Giacometti, which cost me 50 euros. It was another item that really said something, a sculpture that had been welded together out of nuts and bolts and then cast in bronze. Why would someone do that? That's what interested me. Almost certainly because nuts and bolts were the only materials they had to work with.

The deeper we got into the place the larger the shops became. Now they were no longer just cubicles, they were a decent size packed with stock, and we stopped at one that looked about 15m square. At first glance it didn't seem very promising; the only thing that attracted me was a light hanging in the window. But when we walked in, it was like – *bang!* We were with somebody who really knew their job.

The sign outside said Pieta & Pieta and the owner couldn't speak any English. My Hungarian doesn't stretch further than the word 'Hungary', so we had to find a way to communicate. At first, there was nothing to say, because the quality of his stock just hit me and I had to take that in before we could strike up any kind of conversation. It was world class, chosen by a really intelligent, educated eye, and I was completely taken with it. Equally, I was wondering what a guy with this kind of education was doing in a place like Ecseri – no offence meant, of course, it just seemed so incongruous. The way he had everything displayed was really clever and thoughtful. It was something that takes a well-practised eye and a real understanding of the business. I could tell he'd been in the trade for a very long time and I was desperate to ask him about it. Like a kid in a sweetshop, I just started buying things: sculptures, bronzes, art and furniture, as well as a pair of hairdressing scissors in the Ascetic style, which I recognised because my auntie had been a hairdresser.

The more I bought, the more I wanted to talk to him. But we couldn't exchange a word and yet we had so much to say because we were coming at the same subject from completely different worlds, and yet with a commonality between us. A classic example of a shared passion that straddled completely alien cultures. I knew nothing of life in Hungary, either before or after Communism, and he had no idea what it was like to grow up in Glan Conwy. I wanted to know if he'd taught himself to appreciate the history and beauty in the same way I did, or had he been tutored by someone. We had such a similar eye there were bound to be things we had in common, so not being able to discuss them was incredibly frustrating. He reminded me of Jon Tredant, a man we were going to see the week after we got back to the UK. Old school, proper, knowledgeable: if you look up 'antique dealer' in the dictionary, you might see the definition as 'Jon Tredant'. He's a man who's been knocking around about as long as I have, and I had the same feel about that guy in Ecseri.

It was hard to communicate with any real authority. Lazlo did his best to interpret but so much gets lost in translation. It was a pity, but tempered at least by the quality of the stuff I was buying. Normally when we're buying in a flea market, T and I might spend ten minutes at a stall before we move on, but we were at least an hour and a half with this guy. As Olly said afterwards, I put my glasses on my head and descended into silence, and when that happens, he knows we're in for the long haul. As I said, the shop wasn't very big, but it was packed with such fantastic stuff I was immersed from the moment I stepped inside. He had a female marble bust from the Communist era, something I'd never seen before. That's the time to buy, but he wanted 600 euros so I passed on it and I don't know why; the bust would be three grand on the website and I was spending thousands anyway. I bought masses of other stuff, though, including four superb cigarette cases that had been gifts for the upper echelons of the Communist Party. They were just brilliant so I snapped them up at 300 euros for the lot when one alone would easily fetch that.

Finally, we had to move on, and I was still gutted that I hadn't been able to get to know the guy, but that's the language barrier for you. We took a look in the place next door where the dealer told us he'd cleared every Communist hospital after the Russians went home and left everything. Cabinets, tables, chairs; I bought his entire stock and picked up a pair of donkey-ear trench binoculars that were used for range-finding. Like a periscope, there's a series of mirrors that allow you to see over the top of the trench so you don't have to risk getting shot by sticking your head up. This was NOS (new old stock) that had never been used and was marked 'Made in 1950'. The case was missing, but the binoculars came with the tripod and both were in mint condition. The dealer also had some desktop toys made for the top brass that really appealed to me. Oddments, the kind of thing I'd not come across before and could only be bought from a place like Hungary. There was a train, a MiG fighter and the weirdest thing ever. I picked it up and it took me a moment to work out that it was a missile launcher. This was a real insight into how things must have been during the days when the Soviets ruled here. Beautifully made, the missile launcher was cast alloy that had been painted, with the rockets in chrome sitting on top of it. It was set on a multiple-wood timber base with an alloy inset and it was up for 50 euros. As I parted with the money, I imagined some high-ranking Russian army officer with this on his desk as he supped vodka and smoked Belomorkanal cigarettes.

It was an amazing glimpse of how the Soviet Union was so steeped in militarism they made missile launchers as desk toys to give to their officials. That was a first, but I already knew that back in the 1950s they used to make models of TV and radio towers, which have since become highly collectible. They're every bit as beautifully made as the launcher; 45–60cm tall, cast in alloy with clear plastic sections and timber bases, it's craftsmanship at its finest. Back then people in the Soviet Union would make long trips to visit the sites of the real TV aerials and come home with a model. I knew about that, so I started buying them up whenever I saw them in junk shops or on eBay. There are only so many out there and by the time I was finished I had a collection which I put on the website and sold in its entirety.

It had been an incredible first day and, after we packed up the gear, we piled back to the hotel to take a shower, then headed for that cheap bar I mentioned next-door to the hotel. We called it 'The Spoons' and got absolutely fucked on 50p pints of quality lager. We weren't working tomorrow, Saturday was a rest day; we were heading out on Sunday and were all full of the events at Ecseri. It was as perfect a start to any overseas trip as we'd made. I was in love with this place; the variety and quality of the antiques I'd bought would add a whole new dimension to our website. I spent Saturday organising shipping and liaising with Ruth and Michaela back in Conwy. They run things for me, make sure the money we bring in is taken care of, and ensure the whole operation runs like clockwork. I couldn't do what I do without them. Ruth sets up my entire life and I have no idea where I'm going or what I'm doing until she tells me.

That evening Olly took us to the food court at Szimpla Kert, where I had the best cheeseburger I can remember. I love cheeseburgers, one of my favourite things to eat, and this was as good as any. I've eaten in some top-notch restaurants all over the world but, if you get a good cheeseburger, there's nothing to beat it. After that we headed for a 'Ruins Bar'; they're dotted all over the old Jewish quarter.

They're called 'Ruins' because this part of the city was badly bombed in the Second World War and very few residents ever returned to their homes after. For years the area was left derelict, then the Berlin Wall came down and a few young mavericks reconditioned the empty buildings into eclectic 'Ruins' bars that are famous all over the world now. Courtyards stuffed with tables, balconies, shabby high-ceilinged rooms that have never been repainted, they were beautiful. It was just another facet of what was fast becoming a favourite city.

Heading southeast towards the Romanian border on Monday, we spent a few days on the road guided by a dealer called Balacz, who was running for mayor in the town of Vac close to the Slovakian border. That would be our last call before we flew back to Britain. In the meantime, we called on lots of places, where we found a raft of Soviet-era stuff, including industrial furniture. The language was pretty impenetrable but, as that week went by, I slipped into a rhythm of hand signals and the odd word from our interpreter. The contributors were great, but Balacz was going to be a long-term contact. He took us to an old grain mill where I picked up tons of stuff to add to what I already had. Most of it can best be described as house clearance, sort of Communist Bloc stuff that was beige and horrid and cheap, but there were a couple of engineering gems that were both architectural and industrial.

Balacz was really knowledgeable and a dealer I could connect with. He and I struck up a friendship right away and he told me he lived in a castle he bought for nothing when the Soviets moved out and everybody else moved in. Among his stock were lots of bits and pieces that made up architectural shop fronts, and I bought an entire façade for 650 euros.

On the way north again, we stayed the night at the most beautiful spot on the Danube after exhausting our collection of sing-along country music like one big happy, gypsy family. It personified the trip; outside Budapest the food had been terrible but the accommodation great and the company of Hungarians warm and friendly. The beer was cheap, which helped oil the wheels, and I was looking forward to seeing the last place Balacz had arranged for us to visit. As far as we could tell, it was the largest antiques warehouse in Hungary and run by a guy called Zsolt, which is pronounced Jol-T. I wasn't sure what to expect but he turned out to be one of the most switched-on people I've met and another guy I'll continue to do business with. When the lads arrived, he had schnapps and coffee waiting. This was 7:30 in the morning, but, apparently, it's the custom and if you don't partake it's very rude; so, of course, we all obliged him. Previously an old Soviet concrete casting factory, the place was so big Zsolt had motorised scooters for his customers to get around on. I kid you not, they were lined up before we got to the schnapps and we needed them because this place was enormous.

I bought everything from industrial ceiling lamps to an array of incredible furniture, including cupboards and cabinets, small tables, large tables, benches, stools and a whole array of glass hospital cabinets, as well as two massive wall signs. The place was stacked floor to ceiling with antiques, with a series of offices above accessed by metal stairs and walkways. I don't think I've ever seen such an eclectic range in any one place. Just about everything you can imagine was being sold, from ornaments and furniture to scooters, motorbikes and old bicycles, even a couple of horse-drawn carriages. It was one of the best days I've ever had buying. The flea market had been great but this was on another level. On top of the other stuff, I picked up a pair of folk-art dragons to fit on the end of water spouts and an eighteenth-century carriage seat. There were console tables, a marriage cabinet and a wonderful old zinc bath, as well as a couple of heavy industrial pieces that had been part of the casting factory. Having bought so much, I'd already upped the size of the van to ship it home to a 10-tonne truck, but I still wasn't finished. When the crew stopped filming, I carried on and bought another entire collection of medical cabinets.

It was a wrap, the Hungarian adventure almost over. We had a last meal on the banks of the Danube and reflected on a massively successful effort. Everyone had worked so hard, the hours for the crew were insane, and I'd had to be on it all day every day. Now we were leaving, it felt like a huge comedown and the change in atmosphere was tangible.

It's an incredible thing I get to do. I travel the world meeting new people and buying beautiful things and I consider it a blessing, really. I know how lucky I am, but to be that lucky you have to work very hard and I'm on it 24/7. In the casting factory alone, I bought 39 different items and within that there were multiples of nine. I'd spent ten grand, which pushed the total for the trip well beyond £40,000, but I knew I'd get most of it back in the first few items that hit the website.

I had a lot to reflect on and not just the quality of what I'd been able to buy but the country itself, the people and contacts I'd made that would be great for future business. Balacz understood the kind of thing I was looking to buy, and if something really good came up, I knew he'd be on the phone to tell me.

CHAPTER 11

T'S A COCKNEY GEEZER

In the morning, I left Hungary for Manchester with Carl and Simon Jolly, each of us carrying a couple of large batteries. There are so many required for a shoot like that, they can't all be shipped as one unit, so they're split between us for the journey.

The flight was only two and a half hours and I took a moment to close my eyes and reflect on a really great buying trip, particularly that graphite on paper, which was my personal highlight of Budapest, something I would keep. There have been a few such items down the years and I've mentioned some, but there's one that stands out above all the others: a wall frieze from Thomas Bruce, the 7th Earl of Elgin, who removed half the surviving Parthenon sculptures from the *propylaea* (temple entrance) at the beginning of the nineteenth century. Classical Greek marbles, they were designed by the architect and sculptor Phidias 2,500 years ago.

What made Elgin think it was alright to bring them back I don't know, but it caused a storm when they were shipped to Britain, with luminaries such as Lord Byron claiming it was an act of vandalism. In 1798 Elgin had been appointed as ambassador to Selim III, Sultan of the Ottoman Empire, who ruled over Greece. Before he left, Elgin asked the British government if they were interested in sending out artists to draw and cast the marbles. They weren't up for it, and whether that inspired him to bring the originals back instead, we'll never know. But the fact that he'd thought of taking casts had always been of interest to me. I'd read about Elgin years ago and I knew he'd not taken any casts in Greece because he acquired thirty-odd metres of the frieze instead. According to the research I'd done, though, when he got them back to London, he made two plaster casts of each individual piece and had them framed very simply.

So, I knew of the existence of casts, but I'd never actually come across them until one day when we were filming at a private girls' school down in Sussex. I can't remember where it was exactly – T will know – I just recall we'd been filming and picked up a few items, though nothing that really set the juices flowing. Old schools can be a good source of material and you never quite know what you're going to find, but we'd exhausted all possible areas except a couple of junk-filled garages.

They were stacked with defunct cookers and old washing machines, some doors and bits and pieces of shite, and we were about to call it a day when I noticed something about the way the floor was constructed. It was on two levels, one considerably higher than the other, and right at the back was some old furniture we were yet to go through, so I poked around a little. At the point where the floor met the wall the gap seemed a little over-wide and I realised something was stored there. Whatever it was had been stacked like crackers in a package so it was vertical; I could see what I thought was the corner of a piece of plaster about five centimetres deep and there was something unusual about it. The sixth sense I've cultivated since I was a kid kicked in, and I felt a tingling sensation.

'Hey, T?' I called. 'Come over here.'

He made his way to where I was standing.

'Can you see that?' I said. 'It's some kind of frame. That corner is definitely plaster.'

'D'you want me to get it out?'

'Can you? I mean, without breaking it?'

'I can try,' he said, and set about attempting to work it free.

Whatever was back there, it was pretty long and pretty deep and, as T began to lever it free, I could tell it was a large plaster casting. He got it to the point where I could take the other end and, between us, we started to drag it clear. It wasn't easy and we had to be careful. We had to move old doors and other bits and pieces to make sure we didn't damage it and it was only then I realised just how big it was. We had to slide it clear, so T took hold of his end and I leaned against the wall so I could push the other end with my foot. It was bulky and very heavy and my bad back had been killing me all day. I've got this disc that likes to pop out now and again, often when I'm in a car … and I'm in a car for long periods.

So, T did the donkey work but I helped as much as I could and we managed to get it free. It was facing the wall and I still didn't know what it was, but the way the frame had been constructed really intrigued me. This was some kind of frieze and the nails that held it to the frame looked right for the period. On closer inspection, I could see the same was true with the construction of the timbers themselves and the way they had been jointed. My mouth was dry and a surge of adrenalin seemed to rush through me. I thought I knew what it was and, when we turned it face on, I was certain. The frame, those nails, the way the timbers … I couldn't believe what I was looking at.

'Fucking hell,' I said.

'What is it?' T said.

I had my glasses on my head, standing with my hands on my hips. I looked it over very carefully.

'What is it?' he repeated.

'It's part of the Parthenon Frieze, cast by Lord Elgin when he brought them back from Athens.'

'You're kidding me.'

I was shaking my head. 'He made two of every section and I'm positive we're looking at one of them.'

It wasn't in the best of shape, a little damaged in places and damp from having been stored in the garage. I'd seen plaster reliefs like this go for three grand at auction, but not one of the marbles taken by Elgin. I was pretty sure this was one of his casts but I'd need to have it verified. Technically the history was questionable so I had to hedge my bets when it came to what I was prepared to pay for it. With that in mind I offered the school 1,600 quid, expecting them to come back at £2,000. But they didn't. They shook my hand on the £1,600.

Since then I've taken some flak online with people claiming I ripped them off, but I didn't. I thought I knew what I was looking at, but could not be sure, and £1,600 was only my opening gambit as none had been on the market before. Given the frieze was beginning to rot, the value would only go down the longer it sat there and it had already been hidden away for years. The school accepted the bid so I wasn't going to up it, but I'd already paid over the odds for the rest of the stuff I bought from them anyway. It's important to remember that the things you see me buy on TV are only what we can fit into that 15-minute slot, and some of what I come away with is purchased off-camera. I picked up plenty that day and paid handsomely for it, so we all won.

I love that cast and still have it at home in Conwy. It's my favourite thing in the house and I thought it was worth three grand all day long, and it still might be. But this business is fickle, and recently three similar pieces went through an auction house at only 600 quid. Those were also Elgin casts but smaller, and not the size of the originals. I think the price I paid was a fair reflection of condition and provenance. Right now, I'm not selling, but I still think I'll make money when the time comes because mine is exactly the same size as the original. I haven't had an expert out, but the nails are handmade and were manufactured around the turn of the nineteenth century, which was correct. The joints, the way the whole frieze was put together, tell me I wasn't wrong and the one I have was made by Lord Elgin. As a decorative object it's just fantastic. I know which piece of the Parthenon it is; I've been to see the actual marbles and checked every last detail. What bugs me is not the price the others were sold at, but the fact that I missed them. I only found out after they were gone, and if I'd known they were going under the hammer I'd have bid on them.

Elgin's removal of what were actually the 'Phidian Marbles' spawned a neo-classical British take on what the Greeks had been doing more than two thousand years previously. That era formed a period in architecture and design that's never been equalled and I'm proud to think I have an original cast in my collection.

Back home from Hungary, I barely had any time at all before I was on the road again, heading for the Cornish/Devon border. Things had been so hectic I'd not had a moment to think. One day seemed to merge with the next and I had to count back before I could figure out this was Wednesday. Ahead of me was a five-and-a-half-hour drive without stops and traffic, so it could be as bad as seven. That's the worst bit of the job, but it has to be done if I'm to find the most interesting places and people.

I was tired before I even got started. Early in the week someone had hacked our bank account and stolen £14,000 before we were able to put a stop to it. It was something I could've done without, and there had been some other personal stuff flying around that I put down to bullshit stories peddled by a local rag of a newspaper whose name I won't bother to mention. Suffice to say, the crap they've printed over the years has caused me untold problems; sometimes living in the place where I grew up can be a real hassle. Every now and again it gets a little crazy and there's a part of me that yearns to disappear off to Italy or buy a flat somewhere nobody knows me.

In-car time, though, there's an awful lot of it, and lately I've been travelling alone on the way to shoot the TV show because T now lives a long way from Conwy. Whereas we used to take off in the van together, we can't always do that any more; sometimes we don't hook up until we get to the destination. Today I was in the Range Rover, which is a nice place to be, but I've put 72,000 miles on the clock in the 18 months I've had it. That's without van time, so you can see just how great the distances are we have to cover. Despite being knackered, I was looking forward to Dingles

Fairground Heritage, which was the call we'd make tomorrow. It was 2:30pm already and I was only just leaving Colwyn Bay but I had my office on wheels and my music. At 5:00pm I'd put on Radio 4 and listen to the news before the comedy half-hour at 6:30. That's sacrosanct, no matter where I am or what I'm doing, that's time I have to myself every day and nothing gets in the way of it. I switch off at 7:00pm because I can't stand *The Archers*, but I have to listen to the comedy.

After a night in another hotel, we spent a mad day at Dingles, which was something of a landmark moment. Just shy of ten years ago, we visited the place on the very first series and turned up (all of us and all the gear) in a single people carrier. A rabble, that's how Simon Jolly described us. Not really knowing what we were doing but full of enthusiasm anyway.

Dingles is an entire fairground that two old boys put together to create a heritage centre that's also used by schools as an educational facility. As Simon said, it was like gate-crashing an episode of *Scooby-Doo* where we showed up in our very own 'Mystery Machine' and were confronted with all the old rides and music. Ten years later we were back, and we were a little choked up with emotion. Neither Simon nor I had believed we'd come this far; for my part I'd never contemplated the idea of a second series, let alone still doing it ten years later. But the fact is we're still here and that's largely due to Simon. He was the one who saw the way I was in front of the camera and told me just to keep on doing what I was doing. Back then I was getting a little bit of flak from the producers because (despite the leeway Philip had given me) I was too honest and upfront, and they wanted that tempered a little. Simon didn't agree and he stuck his neck out to tell me. In fact, he could've got fired for what he said when he nudged me one day and told me it was really good and to ignore what everyone else was saying. That made up my mind and it's how I've done the show ever since.

To be back here where we'd filmed during that very first series resonated and we were both more than a bit nostalgic. So much had happened since; people had come and gone, and others had taken their place. Children had been born and some of us had been through messy divorces. All the while, though, the show grew in popularity and the only real constants were me, T, Simon Jolly and Gavin.

With nostalgia still trickling through our veins, we arrived at yet another hotel, then most of the crew went out for a curry at an excellent Indian restaurant in Exeter called Ganges. Afterwards we sat down for a drink and Simon and I reminisced about all we'd accomplished over the last ten years of the series. The beer was flowing, as were the war stories, when a guy came over to say 'hello', and he seemed to immediately personify all that we'd been trying to achieve with the telly. His name was Gary Churchward and he was in the bar later than he should have been, having promised his wife he'd be home by 11:00pm. It was well past that already and he still had a 20-minute walk ahead of him. He'd been about to leave when he spotted us rabble as we came through from the restaurant and decided to come over and introduce himself. A really nice guy, he was a fan of the show, the second person to tell us that night. Gary's been a guard on the railways for 32 years and was into railway memorabilia long before he started watching the series. He told us he'd been watching since the very beginning and, after he'd gone, I looked long and hard at Simon.

'Sums up everything we've been through today,' I said. 'Ten years on and who would've thought it?'

I know there are thousands of people out there like Gary whose interest in antiques has been taken to another level because they've watched the series. What really grabbed him was the time I came across a set of stacking (or modular) bookshelves made by Globe Wernicke, a firm formed in 1899 after Globe Files from Cincinnati bought Wernicke in Minneapolis. I don't remember where I found the shelves, but it was the fact that I knew what they were that piqued Gary's interest. He told me that since then he's done his own research on countless items we've come across and has been completely hooked by the learning curve that goes with the business.

Talking to him was liberating. This was exactly what I'd been trying to do when I agreed to make the show in the first place. Exeter was already special because of where we'd been today and Gary brought that home in a way that was obvious to the entire crew. For that alone the show has been a success, never mind the ever-growing viewing figures. It was the perfect end to a perfect day, only surpassed when we were finally able to flag down a cab big enough for all six of us. The driver recognised T the moment he climbed in and joined us in an Olly-led rendition of that famous old North-Walian ballad: 'T's a cockney geezer, mushy peas and liquor – eels, eels, eels. Eels, eels, eels.'

Yeah, I know – you really had to be there.

Up not so bright and early in the morning, it was back to business and a call to Jon Tredant, the guy I told you about who typifies what it means to be an antique dealer. He runs Carradale Antiques from a warehouse showroom close to Exeter Airport, but we were going to take a look at some of his overflow stock housed in a massive 1870s-built barn in the courtyard outside his farmhouse. The farm itself spans 77 acres and Jon's family moved in on 7 July 2007 – 07/07/07. Prior to that, the house he lived in was number 77, so it's no wonder he considers seven to be something of a lucky number, but it's one of the numbers I have trouble with, along with three and nine. I'm told it's something to do with a form of dyslexia, which wasn't diagnosed until I was 37. Anyway, I was looking forward to talking to Jon; he's a little older than me and wears a pair of ten-quid glasses perched on the end of his nose, though he should go to the optician because he really can't see anything through them.

His history is not dissimilar to mine in that he came to appreciate the business early. When I first met him, he told me how he was dragged around antique shops pretty much from birth and absolutely loathed it. That changed, though, when he was eight years old and made money on a silver fish knife. Since then he's become as obsessed as I am, a real dealer who learned his craft over a number of years and shares my passion for things as 'untouched' as possible. His showroom/warehouse carries a lot of stock that's spread over three floors. He has a good eye and displays stuff with imagination. He's got another warehouse at the same location, plus a few containers he uses to store back-up stock, then there's the farm where the barns are stuffed to the rafters.

'You've got some stock here,' I said, as we climbed the steps to the upper floor of the first barn.

'It's what I call the overflow of the overflow, and there are a couple of pieces I think you might want to have a look at.'

He told me how he'd just put a new roof on the Exeter showroom and was keeping it awash with what he hoped was the right kind of stock. He has a passion for really old, really big cupboards and cabinets, but the market for that kind of thing really isn't there right now, so he's had to hold on to a lot of it. The market will come back, it always does, there's a revolving door to this business, but right now there's not much call for the big stuff. Most of what Jon sells has something going on and it would be interesting to see if the items he thought I might buy would be what I wanted to go for. That's how it works when it's dealer to dealer. We all think we know what someone will want to buy, but this business is full of surprises.

'I like this place,' I told him. 'It's got a great feel.'

'Yes,' he said. 'It reminds me of the farm my mother and father rented and the museum shop I created.'

'You had a museum shop? I was selling bits of old bicycle from the roadside.'

T was already looking around and the amount of stock Jon had on the upper floor alone was mind-boggling. It was packed with dining and club chairs, and tables of various sizes from England and France. There were mirrors, bookcases, even an old wooden canoe upside-down on the rafters. I spotted a grandfather clock and loads of cupboards and cabinets, most of which were early English. He had chairs on desks and a pair of old untouched leather armchairs he thought I might be interested in. We talked about what was selling right now and what wasn't. I pointed out a large carved walnut cupboard dating from the seventeenth century.

'There's another one to match it.' Jon nodded to the far end of the room where an even bigger cupboard was standing. 'I like them, I always have. I bought those in a sale fifteen years ago and they were disassembled. Someone had stored them in a barn since the Second World War and they were in a pretty poor state, but we restored them and put them back together.'

'They're beautiful,' I said. 'A matched pair, it's not often you see that.'

'Schranks, from Bodensee, they're dated 1660.'

'They're good,' I said. 'Really handsome.'

'But too big. Nobody wants them that big these days, but I don't care. I like them.'

I asked him how much he'd paid for them.

'All in all, with the restoration, they cost me £17,000 but I doubt they're worth that today.'

Another buy he'd made with his heart and not his head was a series of Mediterranean fishing floats, green glass spheres strung with thick netting, that were hanging from the ceiling in the stable block downstairs. Jon told me he'd bought a whole stack from a friend of his, years ago, and this was all that was left of them.

'How many did you buy?'

'Oh,' he said, 'at least seven or eight hundred. I regretted it right away and had to work really hard to get rid of them.'

'And what's left here is the profit?'

'Almost certainly.' He had a wry smile. 'I could've sold them a few times since I got rid of the others, but they remind me of a wild deal I made so I'm keeping them.'

I pointed out another cupboard and he told me he'd had that a long time, and had partially restored it. He doubted the market would come back but it didn't matter because the money had long since turned over and it was good background stock regardless. He had a Gothic oak wardrobe and bedroom set that he'd sold to a friend who had recently moved out of the large house where she was living. She phoned him up to see if he wanted to buy them back, and he did, though for only a third of what she paid; but that's how the market was right now so he couldn't give her what she wanted. Jon pointed out that smaller items like jewellery and Rolex watches have done nothing but go up in the last few years, but they're the things you really have to compete for.

I had a vintage Rolex on my wrist that had done nothing but increase in value since the day I bought it. It replaced one I'd been wearing for half my life that came (in a round-about way) from my grandmother Nin, the most important person in my life. She came to live with us in 1973 and was part of the family I grew up in. Winfred Alice Roberts, my mother's mother, she's the reason I'm the man I am today, the greatest influence on my life and the strongest person I've ever met. I said before, five foot of fury but also knowledge and love, and I adored every inch of her. Anything I've ever done is because of her. I don't mean the bad shit, that's my doing, but all the good stuff comes from her. It was she who instilled the 'Take it or leave it – Don't like it don't look' attitude, which I believe has stood me in good stead throughout my career. I don't take prisoners. I don't suffer fools and neither did Nin (or Ninja, as T sometimes referred to her).

When she died in 1992, she left me and my brother £500 each. He bought a Rolex Datejust with the money, but I had a mortgage to pay and nothing to pay it with, so I used her money for a month's worth. A year later I was back at Newark and the guy with the stall next to mine was a watch dealer. He was having a really bad day but he had a very nice Rolex Datejust I had my eye on. He was asking 1,200 quid and I couldn't afford that, but the fair lasted three days and the watch didn't sell, so on the final day I wandered over. 'Show's over,' I said. 'What's your best price on the Datejust?'

'Give me seven hundred quid and it's yours.'

I gave him the cash, took the watch and wore it every single day until I bought the one I have now, because I didn't want to damage it any further. I was 23 then and I'm 49 now and I consider the watch my inheritance from my grandmother. It's stowed away safely now and won't be touched again until it's passed down to my son.

Apart from those club chairs, Jon had a couple of other items in mind he wanted to show me, one of which was a glass tobacco sign he'd forgotten he had because it had been stored behind one of his large cabinets. There was a French farmhouse table he'd only picked up the day before and we'd have a discussion about it. T spotted a really nice English chess table from 1860 made in Verre Eglomise, that's 'gilded glass' where the underside of the top is painted with gold or silver leaf then partially covered in wax before being dipped in acid. That process creates recesses on more than one level, which are then decorated from beneath, giving it a three-dimensional appearance.

All Jon's stuff is quality; he has the eye of someone who's been in the business 37 years; if we weren't filming, I could spend a week here. But we were filming, and the crew was getting restless, so it was time to get down to business.

CHAPTER 12

THE BEST OF
THE BEST

By the time I got back to Conwy after filming with Jon, the lorry-load of stock was on its way from Hungary and I'd already been on the phone buying more antiques. Some of the items I was going to keep (like that pen-and-ink drawing, for example, because for me it was right up there with some of my best finds). There's something about having an item around that's really top quality that is immensely satisfying. It doesn't have to be wildly expensive – it can be as simple as a picture, some folk-art or what looks to some like a knackered old sofa.

The show had come so far since the early days and there's no doubt in my mind that part of the success was down to Rebecca. She's no longer involved in the business, of course, but she and I were together for a lot of years, and, if I hadn't let things slide, it's possible we still would be.

Hopefully, that's a period in my life I've left behind for good, and these days I'm in a much better place emotionally. I'm in a good spot as far as the TV series is concerned, and the business is smashing it. Because I'm writing this book it's been on my mind a lot and the full turnaround I've made since those dark times was exemplified when the quality stock arrived from Hungary. There was so much of it crammed into the warehouse we could no longer get the main doors shut, so whatever had to go to the first floor was shunted up the narrow staircase. Everything had to be photographed and I asked Eleri to begin with the smalls so I could get them onto the website as soon as possible. It would take weeks to get everything we'd bought into the public eye, and I knew I had to get started. That said, we were filming all the time with some big trips coming up, so the upload would be limited to Wednesday and Friday as always. Having cast my eye over the fresh inventory, I left the lads to figure out the issues with storage and drove back to Conwy to repack my bag for the following week.

Spending so many hours at the wheel of a car, I have a lot of time to think (when the phones not ringing, that is), and on the way back from seeing Jon I'd been thinking about this book and everything I wanted to get across. Searching out the best of the best is important to me – it's so integral to this business – and I'd been thinking about some of the other rare and precious items I've found, one of which was an old wooden box.

It wasn't just any old box, though. It belonged to one of my heroes and comes from a period of British achievement that's hard to surpass. Remember I told you I hated boats? Well, that goes for all but one: the *Bluebird K3*, which wasn't the one that broke up when Donald Campbell was killed on Coniston Water, but the one his father Malcolm raced on Lake Maggiore and Geneva when he broke the world water-speed record. Long before that, he'd already broken the record on land at Pendine Sands. A truly amazing man, he was the David Beckham of his era. At 21 he won the first of three consecutive London to Land's End races on a motorbike and by 1910 he was racing cars at Brooklands. When the First World War broke out, he enlisted as a despatch rider then worked as a ferry pilot for the Royal Flying Corps because his superiors thought he was too clumsy to be given control of a fighter. He broke the land-speed record for the first time in 1924 driving a V12 Sunbeam, and in 1927 and 1928 he won the Grand Prix de Boulogne driving a T37A Bugatti. It was on Lake Maggiore in 1937 where his twin-engine *Bluebird* surpassed the world water-speed record that had been set by Garfield Wood in a four-engine boat called *Miss America*. A year later he was back in the boat on Lake Geneva.

Malcolm Campbell had fascinated me since I was a kid and it was well known to my friends in the trade, so when I took a call from a couple of really good dealers I know, I pricked my ears up. John and Jonny from Liverpool, they're good friends I meet up with from time to time, a pair of dyed-in-the-wool dealers who have been in the trade for as long as me. The day they rang I was in the warehouse and I hadn't heard from them in weeks.

'Hey,' I said. 'What's going on?'

'We're at an auction and there's a really special item in the catalogue we think you might be interested in.'

'What is it?'

'Malcolm Campbell's toolbox from *Bluebird*.'

'You're kidding.' I was stunned. 'You're sure it's Malcolm not Donald?' I had to be certain because, if you mention the words Campbell and *Bluebird* in the same sentence, the first thought is Donald and Coniston Water.

'Yeah,' they said. 'It's Malcolm, alright, his name is on the box. It's the one his mechanic used on Lake Geneva.'

That was 1938 and I'd never seen anything like it come up in all my years as a dealer. 'Buy it,' I said. 'Buy it at any cost.'

I owned nothing from Malcolm Campbell and I didn't care how much I had to pay. To this day he remains an icon. A boy's own hero, but a real hard-arse of a guy who didn't seem to have been very loving towards his son. Perhaps that's why Donald was always trying to live up to him, I don't know, but a few years ago I started collecting early photographs of the cars used to break the land-speed record. I had one of Major Henry Segrave, the first person to break 200mph on land in a Sunbeam V12, which was the same car Campbell had used at Pendine Sands. It's a period that really interests me because the most incredible risks were taken with the most amazing machinery. If you see the cars in the flesh, they're mammoth, absolutely terrifying, with no safety aids whatsoever.

So, I wanted the toolbox no matter what it cost, and John and Jonny brought it over a couple of days later. It was a big old thing, planked and painted blue to match the boat and beautifully faded. Malcolm Campbell's name was stencilled into the wood, but the 'Sir' had clearly been added later. He was knighted in 1931 and he hadn't been on Lake Geneva until 1938 so his mechanic must've been using this box long before then. There was no question in my mind that it was the real deal and I wanted it, no matter how much I had to pay.

'How much d'you want for it?' I asked them.

'Twenty thousand pounds.'

Wow, that was a lot of money, especially as I knew they'd only paid £5,000 for it. But that's the trade, they had been there to bid and I hadn't and they knew this was a piece I really wanted.

'How about fifteen?' I suggested.

'No, it's twenty thousand or we're not selling it. It's worth all of that right now. Who knows how much it might be worth if we hang on to it?'

That was a shedload of money for an empty pine box, but it was a magical item. I had to be sure, though, so I gave it another really close inspection. Three things stood out: first, it was marked 'Geneva', which dated it to at least 1938, but I was sure it was used before 1931. It was also stamped with 'No. 1' and that suggested it was the original toolbox Leo Villa (who was Campbell's mechanic) had used on all their projects. I'd never seen another come on to the market, and it might very well have been the box they used on the car at Pendine Sands back in 1924. I'd never be able to prove that, but as well as the fact the word 'Sir' had been added later, there were two shades of blue paint, which denoted the colours of both *Bluebirds* Campbell commissioned. Technically, the box would've belonged to Villa and it looked as though it had also been used to store pots of paint in after he retired. I knew he had worked with both Malcolm and Donald Campbell, so it's possible this box had been used on *K7* as well as *K3* on Lake Geneva.

I had to make a decision, because John's dad (who had been in the trade since before his son was born) had already advised him not to sell it. In fact, he told him he was nuts even at £20,000, so I stepped up to the plate and bought it. Twenty grand for an empty box, it was a massive amount of money, but I've never regretted it for a moment. John and Jonny made a profit and I don't begrudge them a penny. If our roles had been reversed and I'd paid the £5,000, I wouldn't have sold it to them, even if they'd offered the £20,000. It's our job to make a profit and sometimes we're on different ends of that arrangement, that's just the nature of this business. They made good money then and I might make some later. Right now, it doesn't matter. Some things are worth more than money, they transcend profit, and the Campbell toolbox is one of them.

Over the years I've shown it to a few dealers I really respect and none of them thinks I paid too much. One guy who's right at the top of the tree told me it was one of the best things he'd ever come across. He's right. There's a certain magic about it. Look at that box and you don't have to guess at the history, you're there on the banks of Lake Geneva. You're there at Lake Maggiore and Loch Lomond, where *K3* was launched, and maybe even Pendine Sands.

There's been a resurgence of interest lately because of the 'Bluebird Project', where a team of enthusiasts raised the *K7* wreckage from Donald Campbell's fatal 1967 crash in 2001. The boat is now back on the water, having been painstakingly restored to the point where the new one is 90 per cent still the old. I planned to take the toolbox up on the day they first set it back in the water, but we were filming miles away and I wasn't able to do it. I've had various offers for it over the years, none of which I've accepted, though it's on the website if you want to buy it. It's iconic, up there with the sign from the Bugatti factory and the Elgin cast.

It happens with furniture sometimes, too. I've got a Howard sofa in my house that stands against the wall directly underneath the Elgin frieze. It's ratty and old and

I've done nothing to it since I bought it but it's perfect for what I wanted. When I saw it online, I didn't even have to think. I'd been in the house nearly four years and had been looking for the right sofa pretty much since I'd got there. It became an obsession, a bit like trying to find another Porsche after I sold my 911. I found one sofa I thought might work which was up for three and a half grand and I was prepared to pay that, but it had to fit exactly. It was being sold by a dealer I know and I asked to try it before I bought it, but he told me I had to pay for it.

'OK,' I said. 'But if I can't get it through the door it's no use to me. I'm not going to pay for it until I've tried it.'

'Well, you can't try it then,' he said, and that was the end of it.

I was on a mission now, so I sat down with my iPad and started hunting seriously. Literally five minutes later I found the Howard that's now in my living room. The company was started in London in 1820 and became the pre-eminent producers of 'seated' furniture throughout the nineteenth and early twentieth century. It's still going today and remains the best in its field because of innovative designs and the quality of workmanship and materials. It's nice to have something in your home that's considered to be 'the best': I already had two Howard Grafton armchairs and wanted the right sofa to complement them.

As I trawled the net, I found one from 1915 that had seen the kind of wear I was looking for and was exactly the right style. It was unusual because it had been covered by a kilim at the factory. Kilim is a rough type of carpet that fades over time and this had exactly the patination I wanted. I saw it on the Instagram site of another dealer I know, and was positive it would fit, but it seemed to have been on the page for months and I thought he must've forgotten to take it down after he'd sold it. Sure it was already gone, I sent him a quick text message.

You haven't got that still, John, do you?

A message came right back.

Shockingly yes.

How much is it?

To you – £2,600?

Right, I'll have it.

It was perfect: I had no problem getting it into the room and it fitted exactly where I wanted. No adjustment was necessary and I didn't have to move the Elgin frieze. It's in the style of the English country house and I think the best period for that look was around the 1920s. Later on, it was promoted by dealers and decorators like Sybil Colefax and John Fowler. The market quietened down for a while, then in the 1960s it came back with master decorators such as Geoffrey Bennison. More recently, it's been made popular again by people like Piers von Westenholz, David Bedale and Robert Kime. These are dealers who specialise in that really high-end feel and I'm far too much of a magpie to compete, because I have a strong tilt towards the industrial.

My own house, though, is the epitome of that bohemian style and the Howard sofa fits perfectly.

A Howard is the best of the best and, as I said, sometimes it's just nice to know you own something of that quality. It's the same with cars, and for me that's Bugatti or Porsche or the Mercedes AMG GT. Earlier I mentioned that, when I bought an Aston Martin in favour of my 911, I did nothing but regret it after; but for many people Aston Martin is the best of the best and I appreciate that. People love them, they evoke exactly the same emotions as I get from a T35, and every now and again you come across someone who loves them so much they have an entire collection.

During filming for the classic car show in early December, I went on a call to a really rundown area of Birmingham in search of some trim rings for the wheels on a Saab 96 we're in the middle of restoring. J. Hipwell & Sons in Greet is a company that's been supplying specialist car parts since 1898, which is almost as long as the industry's been going. I did a little research and discovered that the first four-wheel petrol-driven car made in Britain was built in 1892 by a man named Frederick Bremer in Walthamstow. The next one was made in 1895 in Birmingham by Frederick Lanchester, who at the same time patented the disc brake. Cars were in their infancy and the company I was going to see were there right at the very beginning.

At their height Hipwell employed about forty staff, though that's dwindled to just a handful. They do a great job; everything is handmade and one of the things I want to do with the classic car show is bring in as many restorers and small businesses as possible. We'd bought this Saab and I wanted to have trim rings (or beauty rings as they were called back in the day) fitted to the wheels to give them that little 'extra'. Trim rings fit to the metal section of the wheel to aggrandise it a little and that's the look I wanted.

When I got to J. Hipwell & Sons, I was met by Paul, a man in his mid-sixties, who told me the company is the oldest manufacturer of trim rings in the world. It was brilliant, perfect, and I have no idea how the lads who work on the car show keep finding these places. Chris, James and Mike; they do an amazing job and this was incredible. An old building that really doesn't look anything from the outside, with one of those old-fashioned plastic 1970s signs where the lettering looks as if it's come off a bag of spangles. Inside, I found myself in a massive Dickensian workshop with wooden offices strung up in the timber A-frame and a floor full of lathes and other engineering equipment. They make air filters and badge bars, but their speciality is trim rings and hub caps, and I told Paul it was trim rings I wanted. Back in the day, Saab were always banging on about their aeroplane technological background and the 96 design was pretty much based on an aircraft wing. It's really fluid and harks back to a bygone era, and I wanted our car to look much older than it actually is. I told Paul I needed the hub cap/trim rings combination to be totally smooth, and he immediately got what I was talking about. We talked about the Saab 96, then he hit me with the fact that he'd made the very last set of hub caps for the very last run of Saab 96s ever made in 1980. Saab UK wanted to go out with a bit of a splash so they came to Hipwell to have the hub caps made specially.

'You're kidding me,' I said. 'You made the originals for the car I've just bought?'

'That's right, a one-piece disc that goes over the whole wheel.'

I couldn't believe it, this was perfect; exactly the sort of thing I'd been looking for. He said he still had some and wandered off to have a look while I took another moment to check out the rest of the workshop. A few minutes later he was back with one of the original discs, still in the wrapping. It had little vents, though, which I didn't want, so I asked him if he could do anything like that and he told me he had another one. Off he went again and came back with one just as I'd described in stainless steel and still in the original greaseproof paper.

I needed four and he could supply that: fantastic, job done. I was delighted. That was all we needed, though, so I turned to go then spotted the wheel of an Aston Martin DBS.

'Why've you got that?' I asked him.

'The wheel? I collect them.'

'You collect wheels?'

'No,' he said. 'Aston Martins.'

I looked at him a little dumbfounded. A Dickensian workshop with just a few people working, in a pretty shitty area of Birmingham. 'You collect Aston Martins?'

'Yes,' he said. 'I've got thirteen of them.'

'What?' I couldn't believe it. 'Thirteen Aston Martins? You don't have any DB4s, 5s or 6s, do you?'

'Yeah,' he said. 'I've got a couple of each. Do you want to see them?'

Of course I did, this was amazing. Paul led me through a side door into a much smaller room but instead of old-school lathes there was an original 1970s V8 Vantage, a DBS and a DBS kit with an alloy body built on the frame of a Vantage. Pulling back a dust cover, he showed me a right-hand-drive DB5 and the hairs stood up on the back of my neck. First made in 1963, the DB5 is the iconic car James Bond drove in *Goldfinger*. Paul told me he races them and, apart from this one, he had another that Aston built for Le Mans but was never actually used. It was the most incredible find in the most unlikely of places. I mean, the area was really run down and this factory a relic from the past, yet here were six of the finest cars ever made. The DBs were stacked on top of each other on four post hydraulic lifts, because there really wasn't enough space for three cars, never mind six.

'God, Paul,' I said. 'You'd have to sell a truckload of trim rings to afford a collection like this.'

'I've had them since the 1960s. When I was eighteen, I wanted to go racing and had the choice between an E-Type for £500 or an Aston Martin for £425. Money was tight, in racing it always is, so I chose the cheaper option.'

He told me he still has that original Aston, and after he went racing, his dad started buying Aston Martins and keeping them. The DB5 on the lift was one of those in metallic blue and absolutely beautiful.

'How long have you had this one?' I asked him.

'Thirty-five years. My dad bought it off a scrap dealer after it'd had a bang on the passenger side so I had to find a second-hand wing.'

'How much did your dad pay for the car?'

'Six hundred quid.'

I asked him how much he thought it was worth now and he told me around £400,000 but it was more like £575,000.

'Would you ever consider selling it?'

'No,' he said. 'None of them is for sale. We didn't buy them to sell. I just love them.'

I got that completely. Paul was an aficionado; he loved to race the cars and that's where the passion began, and it was still the same forty-odd years later. He told me his personal everyday car is a 1966 DB, 3.6-litre with a sun roof and Borrani wheels, which are the sexiest wires ever made and you find them from De Tomaso to Ferrari.

I came away from Hipwell with not just the perfect wheel trim for the Saab, but also an incredible story behind that trim and a whole history of one man's love affair with Aston Martin. It's what makes this job so special and it's why I made the point about the other TV shows and how much they grate with me. It's a special business and what I'd been party to today was just one of hundreds of experiences that this great trade has enabled me to share in. It's ever changing; no two items or experiences are the same and that's why I will always be so passionate about it.

CHAPTER 13

A SPECIAL PLACE TO BE

I spoke about Turner and his relationship to the Modernist movement, but the first time I saw one of his works was a copy my father painted. He really is brilliant, and quite often people would ask him to recreate great paintings such as Turner's *The Fighting Temeraire*. It's an incredibly famous painting that hangs in the National Gallery, depicting the last moments of HMS *Temeraire*, a 'second-rate' 98-gun ship, as it's towed by a tug to Rotherhithe, where it was broken up and used for scrap wood. Turner painted it in 1838 and it was exhibited at the Royal Academy a year later.

I saw my dad working on his version when I was a kid, and remember thinking, Oh my God, what is that? It was utterly brilliant and I just couldn't stop staring. The colours, the way the thin film of cloud is reflected in the water, he captured the whole image so evocatively it stayed with me. Afterwards he took me to a gallery and showed me some original Turners and I was just blown away. I could not believe what I was looking at. The whole visual effect was stunning. Back then I was too young and inexperienced to know why the paintings were so special; now that I do, I'd rather I didn't. The wonder I felt is what got me and sometimes the only way to maintain that wonder is to not understand, just appreciate what you've witnessed. Impressionism in its finest form; Turner was the first to really nail it. As far as I'm concerned, he did it better than anybody else until Van Gogh came along, maybe.

Turner was born in Covent Garden and died in Cheyne Walk, which is where I'd delivered the Empire cellarette that leaked all over that white carpet. By the age of 14 he'd been accepted into the Royal Academy, and was originally part of Romanticism, which was prevalent at the time, and emphasised intense emotion. That was exactly what I experienced when I saw my dad's version of his painting. From what I've read, Turner was a man who retained his cockney accent all his life and when he lectured at the Academy from 1807 until 1828, he was said to be really inarticulate. He travelled Europe in his twenties and you can see the influences in his paintings. He's one of a number of artists I really rate: Hockney is terrific and so is Edward Hopper, who painted *Nighthawks* in 1942. You'll know that if you see it, even if you don't know its name. It's a Modernist image of people at a downtown diner late at night, viewed from the street through a plate-glass window.

Turner was a reclusive figure who didn't have many friends, his best being his dad, who lived with him for 30 years and worked as his studio assistant. He never got married but is believed to be the father of two children by a woman called Sarah Danby. Later he moved into the Chelsea home of the widow Sophia Booth and lived as 'Mr Booth' for 18 years. His work fascinates me. It strikes the emotional chord I've talked about more than any other British artist. We had books about him around the house when I was a child and that's where I did my research.

A few years ago, I was at the National Gallery in Edinburgh where a couple of his paintings hang, and I saw another at a private house in northern Scotland, a castle actually. We were there for an episode of the show, and I got talking about art with the contributor, and told him how much I loved Turner.

'Oh,' he said, 'I've got one here. Come on, I'll show you.'

He had an original hanging on his wall, not the best I've seen, but who cares – it was still a Turner. In his later years he was championed by the critic John Ruskin and, when he died, he left over five hundred oil paintings, a couple of thousand water colours and some thirty thousand drawings. He lived for his art and allowed nothing to get in the way. I love that kind of passion, it speaks to me, and, as far as Turner was concerned, it was born from the copy my father painted. I remember the hazy background; the vision

Turner must've had in order to make it so atmospheric. The flashes of light here and there, it brought the composition to life in a way few other artists have.

It's so much more than a painting, it's a whole other world, a story all of its own and a piece of British history. It's the same with his landscapes, they suck you in so you're right there in the midst of everything. When I look at art, I try to do it from the perspective I had as a child when the whole composition just grabbed hold of me. That's not so easy to do, because the problem with being an antique dealer is that we don't see what other people see, we look at a piece and tend to see the faults before anything else. The best buys are the ones when you don't even have to think about faults; that happened with the drawing I bought at Esceri.

In my opinion Turner is the greatest British artist and I've always wanted to own something he created. The trouble is you can't buy Turner's work, can you? Not unless you've got a few million quid lying around, and I haven't. He left a couple of snuff boxes behind as well as a pair of glasses but you can't buy those either; one snuff box is part of an ongoing exhibition and I've no clue what happened to the other.

So, owning something of Turner's was a desire I thought would never be fulfilled until the day I got an email from someone I'd never met, asking if I'd like to buy his signature. I wasn't sure how they knew I liked him; I suppose it must have come out during an interview. I asked them to send me a photo of the signature so I could see the context and, when it came through, it looked like an entry in a diary or register. I'd have to do some work to find out where that might be from, but in the meantime, I took a long time studying the signature. It looked right, but I'm no expert and couldn't be sure so I sent it to a friend of mine who deals in fine art and asked him what he thought. The response was swift and positive. It was dead right – as far as he was concerned that was J.M.W. Turner's signature.

I immediately rang the seller who told me they wanted £400, and I had no idea if that's what it was worth, but I didn't care. It was worth it to me and that's all that mattered. With certain things there is no top and bottom price, it's all about what it's worth to you emotionally, and for me the emotion attached to Turner far outweighed 400 quid. I was happy to pay, and when it arrived it had that sense of magic about it. This was real and I'd achieved a lifelong ambition to own something by my favourite British artist. Having done some research, I now believe it dates back to his early days at the Royal Academy when he had to sign the register after dropping off a selection of paintings for exhibition. It's one of many signatures on a page from the diary of a well-documented annual event – but it really doesn't matter to me where the signature is from. After seeing my father recreate one of his most famous paintings, I finally had something from the hand of the master.

There have been lots of great British artists, of course, people like Gainsborough and Constable, but there's just something about Turner. When I look at his works, I can appreciate the toil and fight he had with himself to get what he wanted to express onto the canvas. It's what I call 'pure vision'. He knew what he wanted exactly but to be able to recreate what was in his heart like that wasn't easy. I see it in the brush strokes of every painting; the same kind of pain I picked up in the drawing I'd bought at Ecseri.

I understand that toil. I can draw and paint, although to nothing like that standard. When I was restoring stained glass, I would be drawing on a daily basis to design windows and create schemes we would manufacture. I understand the mental process, the way you have to fight to get something you feel out onto the paper. With fine art it's not just the idea, though, it's the entire construction. When I look at a painting, I see the pain and toil, but I also ask myself why the artist chose that particular size of canvas or those specific colours. In the case of *The Fighting Temeraire* I was in awe of how Turner had painted the clouds in such a thin film they looked like gun-smoke. The flashes of light look like explosions. This was a warship about to go to its grave and what he'd achieved was a single picture that brilliantly evoked its history.

That level of appreciation transcends the visual arts into all areas of my life and business. For example, I would put the musician Prince in the same bracket of genius as Turner.

That might sound mental, but in his particular field Prince was exceptional. I've already talked about how the whole mod thing had links to what Turner was doing originally, and the sculptor Henry Moore is up there with him in that respect too. I love Moore's work and have an original piece in my collection. He was born in 1898, died in 1986 and represented all things modern, abstract and surreal. He created the *Recumbent Figure* in 1938 and *Family Group* in 1950 as well as *Nuclear Energy*, which is a domed sculpture resembling a mushroom cloud and is displayed at the site of the world's very first man-made nuclear chain reaction. His stamp is all over that piece, though it's unlike most of the others he created. There's something ominous about it that just shouts at you.

Another guy you can't ignore is the genius that was Rennie Mackintosh, a man who just seemed to pull his work out of nowhere. Originally a water-colourist, he became an architect and designer whose work had links to European Symbolism. He died in 1928 and since then he's been copied and his name plastered over everything from tearoom chairs to shitty stained glass and car stickers. An artist who's been ruined by his own popularity, but if you look at his work, particularly Hill House, Helensburgh, just outside Glasgow, you see absolute genius. He designed the interior as well as the building and most of the furnishings for the publisher Walter Blackie.

It's the same with people like Alberto Giacometti, the Swiss sculptor who created some truly fantastic pieces.

No outside influences, a purity of vision where nothing is watered down, it's the artist at that particular moment, and – for the true greats – that moment spanned a lifetime. I think I've had that level of 'pure me' for about ten seconds in my entire life, but I'm able to get what they're doing and I think that's been evident throughout my career.

It's spanned 33 years so far and I hope it will continue for a lot longer. Year on year I've been climbing, not just in terms of my standing within the trade, but in terms of my knowledge and understanding. It's been a series of steps: you go up one and the next, then another until you get to a level where you stop worrying because you know more than enough to get by now. That's all well and good, but if you keep climbing you keep learning and that way you get to a point you never even knew existed. There the mist just clears and everything is obvious. Your thinking becomes a 360-degree experience. You see things in a completely different way to how you used to and for me that's reflected in houses, clothes, the design of cars, as well as music and the way trends are dictated. When I look at a building, I see how a bricklayer isn't just an artisan, but a visual artist. They have to be, otherwise they'd never be able to get the symmetry and beauty into a particular building. It's not merely the eyes of the architect: it's the vision of the people who actually build it that creates the thing of beauty, and it's the same with a joiner or gardener.

In my case that vision grew as I worked my way up the steps of my career until it all came together in one exceptional, unforgettable moment. A point of acceptance I'd craved ever since I first saw those antique dealers show up at my parents' house to have their vans sign-written. For years I'd held the trade in such high regard, I'd get annoyed when people would tell me they were antique dealers. I knew I was doing ten times the business they were and had a hundred times more knowledge, but I still didn't consider myself to be an antique dealer. Over the years I'd worked on multi-million-pound jobs in hotels and churches, I'd restored old schools with re-creations in stained glass. My whole life had been a constant stream of find, buy and mend old things; but I knew there was so much more to being an antique dealer than that and I strove to get to the point where I could accept *myself*, let alone be accepted.

It finally came to fruition a few years ago when the TV show was into its second or third series. I was 41 years old and we were nailing it as a business. The whole thing was going incredibly well but I still didn't consider myself to be a proper dealer. That changed when I was accepted to exhibit for the first time at the Decorative Antiques & Textiles Fair at Battersea Park in London. This was a way bigger deal than anything I'd done before, including Olympia, which I had done and probably falls into the second tier. Battersea is the crème de la crème when it comes to our business. You have to apply and they vet you to find out if you're good enough and if your stock is up to it. You really have to know what you're doing, have a style or look of your own, so I didn't hold out much hope when I stuck my application in. To my surprise they came back and said I could have a stand, and that was the moment I began to alter the way I viewed myself and my business.

I was a bit nervous because I knew what Battersea meant to the trade and the quality of dealer I would find there. Three days prior to the fair opening, I packed up the van and drove down to London, where I set up my stand. As I was working, I discovered that the dealers around me were the easiest people in the world to talk to. We spoke the same language. We had something in common and, for the first time in my life, I realised I was able to play at the level of most of them.

It was like dawn breaking, and the mist finally cleared for good on the final day of set-up when I walked to the hall through the foyer. In those days the café was off to the right and, as I passed, I spotted Peter Berg, Andrew Purchase, Russell and Mick from 17/21, as well as George from Brownrigg and Paddy Macintosh, David Bedale and Richard Nadin all sitting at one table. These were the best dealers in the country and I wasn't going to stop because I knew they'd have nothing to say to me. I carried on by and was almost back in the main hall when one of them called out to me.

'Hey, Drew,' he said. 'Come on over here. Come and join us.'

I remember thinking, Are they talking to me or is there another bloke in the hall called Drew I haven't come across?

No, there wasn't. Nobody else back there, it seemed that the elite group of antique dealers in the trade were asking me to sit down with them at the high table.

Wow! It was up there with the most important moments of my life and one I will never forget because, prior to that, if someone asked me what I did for a living, I didn't dare say I was an antique dealer, I'd just say I was involved in architectural salvage.

But how you see yourself isn't necessarily how others see you, and as I sat down it became clear that the best of the best had a level of respect for what I was doing that I'd only experienced once before after Alex MacArthur and Ray Azoulay phoned me. I had to pinch myself just to believe I was actually sitting with them. It was so easy, so comfortable, so natural. We were having a laugh, talking about the trade and the upcoming fair and it felt like a bunch of mates taking the piss out of one another and I was completely, deliriously happy. To this day those guys have remained some of my best friends, and I know I could ring any one of them at any time and they would be there for me.

The moment of acceptance, it was so dramatic I could've cried. I knew I was in because if you're going to exhibit at Battersea your gear had better be dead right or you'll be found wanting – and I wasn't.

After that first fair I had the confidence to start mixing in business circles I never dreamed I'd ever be involved with. I found myself in the company of the kinds of interior designers and decorators that cater for the largest country homes and multimillion-pound town houses and apartments. Businesswise I did alright, but when the next fair came around I took £60,000, and the next after that I took £120,000.

After so many years grinding away at the coalface, everything clicked into place and I went up another gear altogether. The moment I'd been looking for all my life; it cemented a fact that I know to be true, though it took a lifetime to get there. I'm not just a man with a van, I'm an antique dealer.

ACKNOWLEDGEMENTS

Jeff Gulvin, Gordon Stewart, Joe Sturgess, my team at DP HQ Ruth, Eleri, Michaela, Neil, David, Sam and all my friends and enemies in the antiques world.

Special thanks to Tee, Paul Cowland, Andy Jaye and Marino Franchitti for putting up with me.

ACKNOWLEDGMENTS

INDEX

271

INDEX

INDEX

INDEX

INDEX